Poetry celebrating the life of

QUEEN ELIZABETH II

From poets around the world

Poetry celebrating the life of Queen Elizabeth II
From poets around the world

Published by THE POET

ISBN: 9798356159527

© THE POET, October 2022, and all the authors herein

W: www.ThePoetMagazine.org
E: Robin@ThePoetMagazine.org

Cover image:
Cover design: Canva

Compiled and published for THE POET by Robin Barratt:

www.RobinBarratt.co.uk

ABOUT THE POET

"THE POET has come a long way; from our very first collection LOVE, in the autumn of 2019, when we featured just twenty-nine poets and 73 poems, to POETRY FOR UKRAINE, our most internationally contributed to collection, with poetry from 254 poets from 53 countries. We now produce some of the biggest international poetry anthologies on particular themes and topics ever published! No matter what your background and experience; whether an established, multi-published poet laureate, with many titles to your credit, or an emerging poet exploring the creative use of words, structure, ideas and expression for the first time, our philosophy here at THE POET is to embrace and welcome all poets, everywhere. Unlike many other poetry platforms, we are not high-brow, nor elitist, nor do we criticize or critique, we are simply a place where poets can both inspire others, and be inspired by others, and a platform where poets everywhere are given an opportunity to have their work published, and their words read."

Robin Barratt – Founder/Editor, THE POET. October, 2022.
E: Robin@ThePoetMagazine.org

ALSO FROM THE POET

We produce some of the largest international anthologies on particular themes and topics ever published.

FAMILY: Volumes 1 & 2
185 poets from 45 countries

POETRY FOR UKRAINE
254 poets from 53 countries

CULTURE & IDENTITY: Volumes 1 & 2
137 poets in 53 countries

ADVERSITY: Volumes 1 & 2
158 poets in 49 countries

FRIENDS & FRIENDSHIP: Volumes 1 & 2
175 poets in 46 countries

FAITH: Volumes 1 & 2
151 poets in 36 countries

CHILDHOOD: Volumes 1 & 2
152 poets in 33 countries

CHRISTMAS – SPECIAL EDITION
97 poets in 34 countries

A NEW WORLD - Rethinking our lives post-pandemic
67 poets in 25 countries

ON THE ROAD: Volumes 1 & 2
121 poets in 28 countries

WAR & BATTLE
54 poets from 26 countries

THE SEASONS
34 poets from 16 countries

LOVE
29 poets from 16 countries

NOTE

We have had submissions to this title from around the world, and for a number of poets contributing to this collection, English is not their first language. Unlike other poetry platforms and publications, we do not heavily edit a poet's own work (*if we did, it would then not be their own work!*), so please focus on the poet's artistic and creative abilities, their styles, and the messages and meanings of their poems for Her Majesty Queen Elizabeth II, and not necessarily on grammatical mistakes or translated imperfections.

CONTENTS

Page:

11.   Mark Andrew Heathcote (ENGLAND)
13.   Joe Kidd (Michigan, USA)
15.   Stephen Kingsnorth (ENGLAND)
16.   Hillol Ray (Texas, USA)
17.   Eduard Schmidt-Zorner (REPUBLIC OF IRELAND / GERMANY)
19.   Santos Kumar Pokharel (NEPAL)
21.   Stephen Ferrett (SCOTLAND)
22.   Michael H. Brownstein (Missouri, USA)
23.   James Aitchison (AUSTRALIA)
25.   Susan Notar (Virginia, USA)
26.   Patricia Furstenberg (SOUTH AFRICA / ROMANIA)
27.   Anne Mitchell (California, USA)
29.   Ledarose Delima (HONG KONG / PHILIPPINES)
31.   Charlotte Langtree (ENGLAND)
34.   Peter W. Morris (North Carolina, USA)
36.   Rohini Sunderam (BAHRAIN / CANADA / INDIA)
37.   Linda Imbler (Kansas, USA)
38.   Ana Atanaskovic (SERBIA)
39.   Clare Starling (ENGLAND)
40.   Zoran Hercigonja (CROATIA)
41.   Rohan Facey (JAMAICA)
42.   Kathryn Sadakierski (Massachusetts, USA)
44.   Catherine Nicolson (ENGLAND / NIGERIA)
46.   Grace Matson (Wisconsin, USA)
47.   Pravat Kumar Padhy (INDIA)
48.   Vanessa Caraveo (Texas, USA)
50.   Dr. Ana Stjelja (SERBIA)
52.   Masudul Hoq (BANGLADESH)
54.   Michelle Morris (ENGLAND / SOUTH AFRICA)
55.   Vyacheslav Konoval (UKRAINE)
56.   Joan Leotta (North Carolina, USA)
58.   Brendon Feeley (ENGLAND)
59.   Lidia Chiarelli (ITALY)
60.   Bernice Baker (ENGLAND)
62.   Vimala Thanggavilo (MALAYSIA)
64.   Jonathan Ukah (ENGLAND / NIGERIA)
66.   Joan Mazza (Virginia, USA)
68.   John Notley (ENGLAND / THAILAND)
69.   Aishwariya Laxmi (INDIA)
71.   Dr. Ivana Knezevic (SWITZERLAND / SERBIA)
73.   Ernesto P. Santiago (GREECE / PHILIPPINES)
75.   Binod Dawadi (NEPAL)

76. Lynette G. Esposito (New Jersey, USA)
77. Sandy Phillips (ENGLAND)
79. Amrita Valan (INDIA)
81. Veronica Roma Pingol (PHILIPPINES)
82. Diana Wickes (Washington State, USA)
84. Anna Ferriero (ITALY)
85. Vicky Walker (ENGLAND)
87. Shirley Smothers (USA)
89. Jason Kirk Bartley (Ohio, USA)
90. Priya Sharma (INDIA)
91. Nivedita Karthik (INDIA)
92. Sarah Law (ENGLAND)
93. Maliha Hassan (PAKISTAN)
95. Kate Young (ENGLAND)
97. TAK Erzinger (SWITZERLAND / USA)
99. Carol Tahir (California, USA)
100. Elisabetta Bagli (SPAIN / ITALY)
101. Bill Matthews (CANADA)
102. Til Kumari Sharma (NEPAL)
104. Francisc Edmund Balogh (ENGLAND / ROMANIA)
105. Liz Grisaru (New York State, USA)
107. G.W. Colkitto (SCOTLAND)
108. Gary Shulman (New York State, USA)
109. Mihaela Băbușanu (ROMANIA)
110. Marilyn Peretti (Illinois, USA)
112. Javisth Bhugobaun (MAURITIUS)
114. Keith Jepson (ENGLAND)
116. Russell Willis (Vermont, USA)
117. Alex Chornyj (CANADA)
119. Manju Kanchuli Tiwari (NEPAL)
121. Dr. Praveen Kumar Anshuman (INDIA)
122. Arun Hariharan (INDIA)
124. Jan Chronister (Wisconsin, USA)
126. Kay Clayton (ENGLAND)
127. Maid Čorbić (BOSNIA & HERZEGOVINA)
129. Rahim Karim (KYRGYZSTAN)
130. Sheryl L. Fuller (Illinois, USA)
131. Hasanul Hoq (BANGLADESH)
132. Francis Muzofa (NAMIBIA / ZIMBABWE)
134. Paul R. Davis (New York State, USA)
135. Charo Gabay Sidon (SINGAPORE / PHILIPPINES)
137. Shabbirhusein K Jamnagerwalla (TANZANIA)
139. Joseph Buehler (Georgia, USA)
140. Shoshana Vegh (ISRAEL)
142. Annamalai Muthusami (INDIA)
144. Robert Leslie Fielding (ENGLAND)

146. Ann Privateer (California, USA)
147. Ion-Marius Tatomir (ENGLAND / ROMANIA)
148. Cathy Hailey (Virginia, USA)
150. Cheryl-lya Broadfoot (ENGLAND / SOUTH AFRICA)
152. Francie Scanlon (New York State, USA)
154. Shereen Abraham (UNITED ARAB EMIRATES)
156. Shakti Pada Mukhopadhyay (INDIA)
158. Tyson West (Massachusetts, USA)
159. Igor Pop Trajkov (NORTH MACEDONIA)
161. Keith Burton (California, USA)
162. Aminath Neena (ENGLAND / MALDIVES)
164. Minko Tanev (BULGARIA)
166. Julie Bonner Williams (Michigan, USA)
168. Chris Nedahl (SPAIN / WALES)
169. Pankhuri Sinha (INDIA)
171. Prof. Mushtaque Ahmed Pathan (PAKISTAN)
172. Margareth Stewart (ENGLAND / BRAZIL / ITALY)
174. Stoianka Boianva (BULGARIA)

QUEEN
ELIZABETH II

21st April 1926 - 8th September 2022

Mark Andrew Heathcote
(ENGLAND)

IN HER DEARLY DEPARTED FOOTSTEPS

Suffused in farewell mists by the river Dee,
the Queen has ventured out to walk the snowfields
alone, far beyond Balmoral Castle one last time,
one last *morra*, and there shortly after the next
she'll-depart-these her well-loved Scottish glens
like so many a rare red bushy-tailed squirrel.
And the world that she cheered and warmed
many centuries hence shall be hushed - husheD
into a shocked silence, petrified as she leaves
the stone steps of her throne, sullen and icy cold.

As her footsteps, leave-us-all, solemnly-behind
we see the rabble and the gentry huntsman bowing
their-lowly-heads in kind. Our noble Queen
has trodden a path that has never frozen,
wavered or forked her pristine footprints
never stumbled, never soiled stained-the-ground
they a tightrope walked. They melt away still pristine
from-us-now one and all. As tears like suspended-
tiaras earnestly heartfelt fall. Her hounds are
heard-baying - howling frantically in the grand hall.

Now her walking cane isn't needed anymore
Now that the mantle of her crown
courts another-rightful son and heir.

Now she waves goodbye with a regal wave of
her royal hand. And all her subject's remarks
she-ruled-our-land with grace and dignity
that no other could likewise command.
Your Majesty, we loved you dearly and would all
take an oath on the stand and there proclaim
she loved all her people, all her subjects
in equal proportions, living in however many distant lands.
God, Save the Queen and God-guides-all-of-mankind,
humankind in her dearly departed footsteps.

*"I do believe most people in difficult situations daydream and go to
their happy place, so here I'm imagining Queen Elizabeth II on her*

11

deathbed walking to a frequently visited loved place. Strolling-beside riverbanks she so dearly loved, near weightless, like an orb of light in the-midst-of-wintertime. I imagine her ethereal body like a feather carried, never having put a foot wrong, vanishing into the mists without any footprints to follow. Taking a stroll that would have been familiar as a morning walk, simply never to be seen again."

~

Mark is adult learning difficulties support worker. He has poems published in journals, magazines, and anthologies - both online and in print - and is the author of *In Perpetuity* and *Back on Earth*, two books of poems published by Creative Talents Unleashed.
E: mrkheathcote@yahoo.co.uk

Joe Kidd
(Michigan, USA)

THE QUEEN TONIGHT

Here lies our Queen in great robes of splendor
scent of roses fill the thick fragrant air.
No breath now sweetened with Indian tea
to wash down the scone, moist and glazed.
The road before her, short and sorry,
the bejeweled crown so ornamented.
A relic encased and put away
among the lamentations sung.
No mercy for departed glory.

A nation born in a darkened past
chooses to line along the path.
But neither smile, nor wave, nor whisper
to acknowledge the tear upon a cheek.
The witness shall recall the day,
retell the tale as if it be true,
of every kind word and each gentle movement
directed toward a populace
of grief and wonder at lost times and thrones.

To be buried thus below these stones
forever bowed around such quarter,
and so the offspring collect the dust.
A feather falls before the sovereign
to pocket and to memorialize.
Final chance, this moment, to join the procession,
to deploy the guard forever loyal and brave.
Brutal fate befallen in royal succession

"What exists beyond the normal and the natural, has always been my affection and respect for Her Majesty. Her consistent presentation of calm grace and elegant reserve. We have witnessed her growing old along with ourselves. Now she has disappeared into the parade of souls, as we all shall eventually follow. Queen Elizabeth was poetry itself, in motion as has been said. It is my effort here to add a personal thought, and to say good bye. To offer a small public testimony of one person saluting as the cortège passes by."

~

ABOUT JOE:

Joe is a working, published poet and songwriter, touring North America and Western Europe. In 2020 he published *The Invisible Waterhole,* a collection of spiritual and sensual verse. His work is found in countless anthologies, magazines, and websites. He has been awarded by the Michigan Governor's Office and the US House of Representatives for his work to advance Peace, Social Justice, and Cultural Diversity. Joe is a member of National & International Beat Poet Foundation (USA), Society of Classical Poets (international), Angora Poets (Paris France), and 100,000 Poets For Change (international). Joe was recently installed as Official Poet of the Government of Birland.

FB: @100063704010587

Amazon Author Page: @B089QYDXSM

Stephen Kingsnorth
(ENGLAND)

AMONGST THE WAVES

I saw her in the Maundy aisle
of steady stream, robed city life,
my viewpoint from cathedral stall.
So short beneath the vaulted heights,
but stature tall as gazed about,
an eye caught from amongst the crowd,
sight, finite, felt infinity.

I have the invitation card,
calligraphy in serif styled,
but on the day for charity,
she suffered cold, did not appear;
with faithful Philip, met instead.
And so her daughter, Princess Royal,
and Prince, now King, those years ago.

But Monarch then, in violet haze,
amongst the waves, her people, sea,
a gracious isle of dignity,
against dull dun of polished tiles,
our Queen alone, purple in aisle.

"I was privileged to speak with the Duke of Edinburgh at an Action for Children charity event; Prince Charles in Warrington after a bombing in the town; Princess Anne at a service I led on the 25th anniversary of the tragedy. As Freeman of the Borough of Warrington, I am invited to the local proclamation of the former Prince of Wales as King Charles III. But, as a member of the Cathedral Council, first seeing the Queen at Liverpool Cathedral on her Maundy Thursday visit, remains outstanding."

~

ABOUT STEPHEN:
Stephen has a Cambridge M.A in English & Religious Studies. He retired to Wales from ministry in the Methodist Church due to Parkinson's Disease. He has had pieces published by on-line poetry sites, printed journals and anthologies.
W: www.poetrykingsnorth.wordpress.com

Hillol Ray
(Texas, USA)

EPITOME OF LOVE AND FRIENDSHIP

Shadows beneath the shadows change,
Ar the turn of the lights-
And bring us joy or sorrow,
As we feel in our sights!

"Elizabeth", you stood like an epitome of strength,
With a motivation for all-
And offered helping hands through thick and thin,
As if at the beck and call!

Today, you left us with a deep void,
In the waves of our love and friendship sea-
And my saddened heart is trying to say:
Au Revoir! Elizabeth! I will miss Thee!!

"The history of United Kingdom, particularly the King and Queen stories, always enchanted me from my childhood. I have read and heard so much about Queen Elizabeth II in my lifetime, that her memories and contributions are unforgettable. The best way to pay my tribute to her was to compose this poem with personal feelings embedded into it."

~

ABOUT HILLOL:
Hillol (D.Litt., Ph.D. Honoris Causa), is a poet, author, and songwriter, and is employed as a Civil-Structural and Environmental Engineer, with the U.S. Environmental Protection Agency (EPA). His poems have been published nationally and internationally, and he is listed in *Marquis Who's Who* in America, *Who's Who in Science and Engineering*, and *Who's Who in the World*. Recently published books include: *Darkest Hour to Ivory Tower* (Autobiography), and *Wings of Time*.
E: Ray.Hillol@epa.gov
FB: @ray.hillolk

Eduard Schmidt-Zorner
(REPUBLIC OF IRELAND / GERMANY)

A ROYAL MOTHER

London falls into darkness,
a low on the kingdom descends,
like an icy winter that freezes tears,
melted by the warmth of the hearts
of people lining the streets,
waiting in endless rows,
respectfully,
for the Queen's coffin to pass by.

Ich Dien, her motto, until her end,
a profession taken seriously,
tireless, steadfast, and responsibly.
She never lied and never betrayed.
Service in life, hope in death.
A mother for her country,
endless.

Motherly feelings, motherly love,
for her own family
and for the family of nations
over the sea and oceans,
over vast and small islands,
Scottish Highlands, Welsh mountains,
English parks and castles,
and lush Irish pastures.

She ruled and calmed the waves,
though politically restrained,
mediated, sought reconciliation,
and practised forgiveness,
an example for all of us.

I remember the outreached hand
to a country which was expelled
from the communion of nations,
deserved, on its knees,
but she opened the hearts,
brought people together,
asked for understanding and tolerance,
as a mother does

with a bunch of unruly children,
with understanding, empathy, and tact.

She was loved, at least respected,
her efforts recognised and admired.

The funeral procession rolled
through London, she, one last time.
142 marines pulled the carriage,
with the Queen's coffin on top.
The spectacular funeral music
by Johann H. Walch was played,
even the instruments fell to their knees
in a musical fall from high to low,
a dramatic *glissando*.

"Death, where is your victory?
Death, where is thy sting?"...
the exuberant question
of believing Christians, like her,
for whom the end
is the beginning.

The atmosphere of the sublime,
death, otherwise a thief in the night
and sleep's brother,
is staged on the streets of London
as a great, awe-inspiring ritual
- a quality, death shares with the deceased.
The crown and death,
they meet in eternity.

She was addressed in church
as "our sister"
a mortal among other mortals,
she became one of us,
a human, a mother, a grandmother
and sister.

The mournful sound
of the bagpiper's lament
swelled and faded in the chapel.
Sleep, deary, sleep.
It was the highest of accolades,
her 70-year reign truly came to an end.

History has now closed a book,

a new chapter begins,
supported from far by her spirit
which is hovering over her people.
We say thank you
and bow our heads.

"Queen Elizabeth II accompanied my life and that of my family and relatives with her historical presence, her dedicated leadership, and tireless, dignified public service. She represented her country in a magnificent way, served as a brilliant example for all of us, and as an anchor and spiritual support for her nation with great understanding for others. I am most grateful to the Queen for reaching out to Germany and Ireland, and for her advocacy of peace and reconciliation."

~

ABOUT EDUARD:
Eduard is a translator and writer of poetry, haibun, haiku, and short stories. He writes in four languages: English, French, Spanish, and German, and holds workshops on Japanese and Chinese style poetry and prose and experimental poetry. Member of four writer groups in Ireland, he has published in over 180 anthologies, literary journals, and broadsheets in USA, UK, Ireland, Australia, Canada, Japan, Sweden, Spain, Italy, France, Bangladesh, India, Mauritius, Nepal, Pakistan and Nigeria, He also writes under his penname Eadbhard McGowan.
FB: @Eadbhard McGowan (Eduard Schmidt-Zorner)

Santos Kumar Pokharel
(NEPAL)

QUEEN ELIZABETH

Her presence will always be noted
Her absence will always do haunt
Her manners will always be quoted
Her greatness is always in count.
Her smile and modest demeanor
Her courteous and enticing charm
Her matters of public honor
Her approach to people was warm.
I had in person not seen her
I live in a distant land
This shall I modestly infer
Destiny! understand.
People say their Eliza
Say people who knew her fine
People say those only heard of
She was a lady benign.
I thought of her royal rhyme
My words will, her eulogy chime.

"This poem is dedicated to the personality of the Queen, her smiling style, her mixing-up with the general public, and her sense of humor that made the environment lively. She descended from the Royal height, and lives in the hearts of the public in many countries."

~

ABOUT SANTOSH:
Santosh is renown award-winning poet, essayist, story writer, a poet and a philosopher and, by profession, a senior civil engineer. Writer of six books, his work has been aired through media in thirty-four languages. His awards include the Anton Chekhov International Award from Russia, the Nikolai Gogol International Award from Ukraine, and the Peoples' Diplomacy Award from Kazakhstan. He is also an awardee of the title Peace Ambassador by World Peace Federation.
E: poetsantosh@gmail.com

Stephen Ferrett
(SCOTLAND)

ADORATUR IN POPULO

Wrapped warm and safe under the Royal blanket, you are the golden thread, woven through the eyes of nations
A blanket of red petals falls from upon high, heads bowed, the bugler sounds the last post.
I look up and gaze for a moment, I glance at the gleaming sparkle of royal tears weeping for those that fell, lest we forget
Emotions are deep and heartfelt, yet, you are stoically strong and proud, the heart of nations beat as one.
Proud, so proud to have given you my oath tenderly young, my allegiance to Queen and Country, like yours, never wavered
Per Ardua ad Astra, Ma'am, you are amongst the stars shining brightly, your spirit once again entwined with your love eternal.

"At the age of 17 in 1985, I swore on the bible along with 20 other young men and women, to serve my Queen and Country after I had been accepted to join Her Majesty's Royal Air Force. The most memorable night when I gazed upon the Queen was at the Remembrance Day parade in the Royal Albert Hall in London in the late 1980s. The emotions were very high on this very special televised tribute to those fallen in WWI and WWII, and was graced by the Queen and other members of the Royal Family."

~

ABOUT STEPHEN:
Since an early age, Stephen has always had a passion for writing and poetry, and has recently published his first children's book, with a sequel on its way.
E: stephen.ferrett@mottmac.com

Michael H. Brownstein
(Missouri, USA)

1981: DEFINING LEADERSHIP

Politics and royalty—pomp and ceremony:
The man stepped from the crowd,
Broke the color of the beauty of the day,
Shot six shots at Queen Elizabeth 11,
And she became the claws of the eagle,
The strength of the panther,
The calm hunter of the night owl.
The birthday parade did not pause—
She did not let it—
And even when the shots were found to be blanks,
She showed a strength in poise,
A poise that was calming,
A calming that created composure,
A composure that yelled across the globe:
Yes, she is the best of England,
A leader with the essence of integrity and courage.

"In 1981, the incident in this poem occurred and I was amazed, then and now, how well she maintained her courage and integrity. In the face of danger, Queen Elizabeth II showed me how a leader should act and react. For this reason I wanted to share this poem honoring her for one of her many acts of great leadership and courage. A great grand lady who showed all of us how we too could and should confront evil."

~

ABOUT MICHAEL:
Michael's latest volumes of poetry, A *Slipknot to Somewhere Else* (2018) and *How Do We Create Love* (2019) were both published by Cholla Needles Press. In addition, he has appeared in *Last Stanza, Café Review, American Letters and Commentary,* and many others. He has nine poetry chapbooks including: *A Period of Trees* (Snark Press, 2004), *Firestorm: A Rendering of Torah* (Camel Saloon Press, 2012), *The Possibility of Sky and Hell: From My Suicide Book* (White Knuckle Press, 2013) and *The Katy Trail, Mid-Missouri, 100 Degrees Outside and Other Poems* (Kind of Hurricane Press, 2013). He is also the editor of *First Poems from Viet Nam* (2011).
E: mhbrownstein@ymail.com

James Aitchison
(AUSTRALIA)

A TALE OF TWO CITIES

They called you "Ma'am" —
but to me, you're "Mum",
although we never met.

I stayed up late to hear you crowned,
on the wireless, through a crackling hiss.
I tried to keep my eyes open
but fell sound asleep; sorry, Mum.

My aunt kept corgis, just like
you did, but my parents wouldn't
let me have one for a pet.
How I begged them!

I went to the pictures and we stood
to attention, before every show began.
And then you and the Duke came to Sydney,
and our school went in to see you.

I told my friends, "She waved to me,"
but they chose not to believe.
I was beguiled, filled with pride,
and that never changed for me.

And when I grew up, I went to London,
saw your palace, your standard flying high.
And one night, police outriders swept beside
my cab, clearing the path for someone …

And there you were, right beside me,
your radiance brightening the night.
I was then I whispered, "God bless, Mum,
I will love you to the last."

"Even though I saw her on only two occasions, Her Majesty the Queen was an inspirational figure in my life"

~

23

ABOUT JAMES:
James is an author and poet who lives in an old goldfields town. His poems have been included in Australian and British anthologies including: *Poetry for Ukraine* and *Culture and Identity*, and a number of poetry magazines including *MindFull.*
E: jimbooks@hotmail.com

Susan Notar
(Virginia, USA)

ODE TO ELIZABETH

You could have left Britain during the Blitz
like so many others
but you stayed home
to fight the Nazi scourge
and celebrated V-E day with your compatriots.

You outlasted all of the men
from Churchill to Blair and Boris
though it can't have been easy
to prove your mettle in testosterone-filled
drawing rooms.

Perhaps you would have been more comfortable
in wellies and tweeds
out of the limelight
by the firelight sipping your gin and Dubonnet.

But with Philip by your side
your beloved corgis trotting at your heels
you provided a comfortable solidity
in a world sadly lacking it.

Leaving us in this 21st century
wondering what is next.

"I was moved to write this poem thinking about her life of service to the UK, and how she must have endured such sexism and yet remained very much a force as she aged. I also liked her sense of humour, for example the video with Paddington Bear."

~

ABOUT SUSAN:
Susan works for the U.S. State Department with vulnerable communities in the Middle East, and has flown over Iraq wearing body armour. She is a Pushcart prize nominated poet whose work has been published in a number of publications including: *Bourgeon, Poets for Ukraine, Penumbra, Burningword* and many others.
Twitter: @susanpoet

Patricia Furstenberg
(SOUTH AFRICA / ROMANIA)

QUEEN LILIBET'S LIFE

Haiku

engines roar amid
serene May bells and corgis-
Queen Lilibet's life

"I wish to remember the woman that was Queen Elizabeth II, this one queen that was also a monarch, and her poised strength as an inspiration for all women that it is possible, it can be done, if you only rise to the occasion. Having it all comes with a price, and a sacrifice is always required, but it is well worth it."

~

ABOUT PATRICIA:
With a medical degree behind her, writer and poet Patricia has authored 18 books about history, folklore, and legends. Her poetry and short stories are published in: *Poetry Potion* (South Africa), *Masticadores Rumania* (Romania), *The Poet Magazine, Spillwords, Lothlorien Poetry Journal, Plum Tree Tavern, Visual Verse, Erato Magazine, Militant Thistles, The Japan Society Haiku Corner, Academy of the Heart and Mind Literary Magazine, Masticadores India, Gobblers and Masticadores* (Spain), *Scarlet Dragonfly Journal* and forthcoming in M*edusa's Kitchen, The Kingfisher Journal, Poetry Pea Journal, Kalahari Review,* and *Cold Moon Journal.*
W: www.alluringcreations.co.za

Anne Mitchell
(California, USA)

POLLINATOR

"The Queen's bees have been informed of her death"

"Please stay", he begs of the broods
while wrapping them in black satin
ribbons, bows to upstage sepias
of September's wildflowers, grasses.

Their keeper knocks
on her hives, offers a prayer
as notice of Her Majesty's death.
Scouts call for a vote,

their waggle dance signals
a resounding "aye"-at Buckingham
they will remain,
but first they gather

for the final swarm,
pageant for their Queenkeeper-
Flight in formation,
bee queens and attendants,

nursemaids, pollen keepers,
wax builders, cleaners and drones-
they join the great queue as it snakes
London's streets, thousands

of her bees alongside
lorrie drives and lords, grans and barristas,
an Indian in eagle feather headdress,
the soccer star, pensioners on walkers.

Camaraderie careens through the final
hush of Westminster's mourning-
curtsey and bow before
the somber luster of her crown,
scepter and orb fastened
in the weight of silence.

"I was so moved by the collective grief of the British people, it was as

though I mourned along with everyone in the country. The observation of ancient ritual and ceremony clearly comforted a nation and brought dignity back into the conversation. I couldn't help wondering what it would be like here across the pond if we had a queen like Elizabeth, someone to dedicate their entire life, in earnest, to serving the people. As an amateur beekeeper, I was touched to read that her bees also mourned."

~

ABOUT ANNE:
A lifelong writer, the year 2020 brought Anne the unexpected realm of solitude, the chance to slow down, observe and befriend words to make sense of this world. Her continued participation in a writing circle serve as both anchor and flame for curiosity to flourish and become poems. Anne's recent work may be found in the *Community Journal* for *writers.com* and *The Poet*.
W: www.Annemitchellpoetry.com

Ledarose Delima
(HONG KONG / PHILIPPINES)

YOUR MAJESTY

A gentle wave of your hand.
A smile shows love you've had.
A voice with authority and deliberate
Touched the heart and painted a smile on each face.

The call of duty.
Devotion for the family.
Only Her Majesty.
Can play that all perfectly.

Your devotion to serve the human.
For all the people under your jurisdiction.
With an open arms and great mind.
Those are the marks you will leave to this land.

The golden rules and laws implemented.
Made others life better and encouraged.
Those people whom you surround.
They are truly blessed, for generously extend your hand.

The sacrifices you bestowed to the people.
The love,care and service to everyone.
Every person who touched by you.
Will be forever grateful because of you.

The world looks the day like night.
The movement of everyone seems so heavy and tight.
Everybody's heart surely fall apart.
Because your light suddenly stops to bright.

Tears keep falling down on each faces.
Just like a child loses their hopes and happiness.
Everybody are broken hearted.
But their love for Her Majesty not be separated.

You maybe gone where we are.
But the legacy you left to this land.
Will remain in everybody's mind.
Your name engraved on humankind.
You will always be our Queen ...

Your majesty ...

"A powerful and sovereign woman, the life of Queen Elizabeth II inspired me to write this poem. I have so much respect for Her Majesty."

~

ABOUT LEDAROSE:
Ledarose is a mother of four children currently working in Hong Kong as a domestic worker. She started writing poems and short stories when she was in secondary high school.
E: ledarosedelima83@gmail.com
FB: @ledarose.delima.7
FB:@black-angel-104784842256532

Charlotte Langtree
(ENGLAND)

QUEEN OF OUR HEARTS

She was always there,
That face almost more
Familiar than our own,
The smiling guardian
Of our home.

And the promise made
Of loyal service,
Of faithful duty and
Lifelong devotion,
Once spoken

With such heartfelt love
For a people who
Loved her in equal measure.
No pledge better kept,
No respect

More well-deserved.
She proved her worth
In time, in commitment,
In untiring obligation
To her nation.

We never thought she'd leave us,
The comfort of her presence
An eternal constant
In a changing world,
The brooch and pearls

As dear as the sun
Beaming from her smile,
And the corgis at her feet:
Memories that shine
Through the march of time.

And we grieve her death,
The loss of the solace
We found in her face
And in her words,

In speeches heard

In times of need.
Through war, through ruin,
Lockdown, loss, and lack
Of guidance, she led
Beyond the dread,

Beyond the fear, she rose,
A symbol of strength,
Of fidelity, of steadfastness,
Experience written in each line on her face;
She was grace.

We joined in gratitude
To celebrate her reign:
Historic, dependable, safe.
Beloved for seventy years
Of laughter and tears.

With sympathy, we watched
Our monarch lose
The ones she loved:
Parents, sister, beloved husband,
Unaccustomed

To life without
Her strength and stay.
He was hers, as she was ours:
The glue that held together, the
Hand to hold forever.

And we join to mourn
Her passing and the empty space
She leaves behind.
In every title worn,
Her Majesty, princess-born,

Lilibet, Defender of
The faith she kept so well,
Queen Elizabeth II
Answered every call,
Mother to us all.

Now we strive to carry on
Without the torch, the
Lighthouse beam that led us home.

In sadness, we hear the muffled bells;
The piper's lament; the last farewell.

Yet, she has earned her sleep,
Global sorrow testament
To her legend.
She has earned our grief,
And the right to rest
In power, and in peace.

"I was moved to write this poem after the sudden death of Queen Elizabeth II, as I was hit by the realisation that I would no longer see a face that had been present all my life. Money, stamps, and Christmas speeches will all change over the coming months but, in writing this poem, I hope to leave a permanent tribute to a monarch whose faithful and steadfast service was nothing less than legendary."

~

ABOUT CHARLOTTE:
Charlotte is a poet, aspiring novelist, and writer of short fiction. The themes of her writing encompass life's all-consuming emotions: joy, fear, love, and loss. She has been published in several magazines and anthologies, as well as online. In September 2021, she was voted winner of the Great Clarendon House Writing Challenge, and Dragon Soul Press selected her story *The Shadow Queen* as an Editor's Pick of 2021.
W: www.charlottelangtree.wordpress.com
FB: @CharlotteLangtreeAuthor
Twitter: @CharlotteLangt5
Amazon Author Page: @B08RX9TGL2

Peter W. Morris
(North Carolina, USA)

GOODBYE OUR ELIZABETH, OUR QUEEN

We were welcomed by the Queen herself
Queen Elizabeth!
As our ship rounded the horn off the Atlantic
Into Sidney Harbour
Australia's world famed Opera House stood
Majestically
Its triangular spires reaching skyward
Adjoining the tallest partition, smiling gently
As was her way
Her Majesty, Queen Elizabeth II
Looked down on her beloved Australia
One last time ...
Days prior to the installation, after 70 years on the throne
This one lady, this one queen, a queen for many nations
Entered her final rest
Meeting, no one doubts, Jesus
Her Savior, the one she claimed throughout her life
Throughout her decades of servitude to a people
Her people of regions around the world
It was right that she should say farewell in this way
To Australians ...
Queen Elizabeth had an affinity with Australia
A constitutional monarchy which she adored
As she loved its people
Sixteen times she had visited this one-continent country
She said she felt a kinship with its "rugged, honest, creative land"
Long live the Queen!
In the hearts and minds of the world's citizenry
Yes!

"Queen Elizabeth II inspired not only her nation, but also nations around the world; multiple countries which had never known a king or queen or royal family to rule over them. As an American, Queen Elizabeth II has fascinated me since I was a little child; one awed at royalty itself. I thrilled at writing about her reign."

~

ABOUT PETER:
Peter has been an international photojournalist and writer since 1970,

when an assignment for the Associated Press found him published worldwide for coverage of Russian fishing trawlers (aka spy ships) in US territorial waters off of New York City. He is the author of 11 books, all centered on his work, which has taken him to over 75 countries on six continents.

E: intlphotojournalist@gmail.com

Rohini Sunderam
(BAHRAIN / CANADA / INDIA)

THE ONLY QUEEN

I couldn't let the day go by
Though I didn't shed a tear or cry
And yet within my heart I know
I grieved because she had to go.
An era ends, an epoch's closed
Her duty's done; she can repose.
For seven decades she has been
In our hearts, the only Queen.

"My connection with Queen Elizabeth is tenuous; I share her birthday. I have always admired her as a person, a woman of immense fortitude and an unflinching sense of duty. To me she embodied the best of the essence of the WWII generation."

~

ABOUT ROHINI:
A Canadian of Indian origin, who resides in Bahrain, Rohini's words have appeared in: *The Statesman, India; Globe & Mail and Halifax Chronicle Herald, Canada; Poetry Rivals* (Remus House). Her books include: *Corpoetry, Desert Flower, Five Lives One Day in Bahrain, Twelve Roses for Love* and the forthcoming *The Missouri Review.* Shortlists and awards include: Atlantis Short Story Contest 2013; Winner Oapschat, UK; Colours of Life, Bahrain; Society of Classical Poets (USA).
W: www.fictionpals.wordpress.com
FB: @RohiniSunderamAuthor
Twitter: @Corpoetry

Linda Imbler
(Kansas, USA)

ROYAL SALVATION

A smiling face,
within these silver walls,
1953,
the newly crowned Queen,
steps from her dais,
exits out the flung open egress,
glides along lily strewn paths,
and comes to meet her Duke.

Together they visit gardens filled with reason,
both antiquated and fresh,
to salvage hope,
and grow more chance for peace
before the world could ever again
feel the last decade's dark.

"This piece was written in homage to The Queen's relationship with Philip. They were already wedded when she was crowned. While she worked for peace, she also had a long and happy marriage. As a result, I felt anything I wrote about her and her later reign would not be as complete without Philip being at her side."

~

ABOUT LINDA:
Linda's poetry collections include six published paperbacks: *Big Questions, Little Sleep, Big Questions, Little Sleep second edition* (expanded with 66 additional poems); *Lost and Found; Red Is The Sunrise; Bus Lights; Travel Sight*; and *Spica's Frequency*. Soma Publishing has published her four e-book collections: *The Sea's Secret Song; Pairings*, a hybrid of short fiction and poetry; *That Fifth Element* and *Per Quindecim*. Her new book, *Rhythms Told*, will be published the autumn of 2022.
Blog: www.lindaspoetryblog.blogspot.com

Ana Atanaskovic
(SERBIA)

TO HM QUEEN ELIZABETH II

You never stood alone
for you had us as well,
us, non-official subjects
who admired your dignity
who tried to be similar to you both in happiness and in sickness
similar to your
purple decency and decorum
purple no-fuss and no-drama attitude
which has now reached the stars.

"I have studied English language and literature for the most part of my life. HM Queen Elizabeth II was the ruler of the country I studied and have admired ever since the beginning of that journey."

~

ABOUT ANA:
Ana graduated English language and literature at the Faculty of Philology in Belgrade in 1997, and has a Master's degree in advertising in literature. As a journalist, she wrote for Serbian edition of *ELLE*, as well as for many prominent Serbian magazines and websites. She also works as a content writer, and has won several awards for best book reviews and stories.
E: anaatanaskovic@gmail.com
W: www.samovoli.wordpress.com
FB: @ana.atanaskovic
Instagram: @ana.atanaskovic
Twitter: @AtanaskovicAna
Amazon Author page:@B004AO1FD8

Clare Starling
(ENGLAND)

I AM NOT READY FOR THE QUEEN TO DIE

I am not ready for the Queen to die
She sits like a small weight at the end of a line
Holding something down

Like Grandma, she does not burden us with her own views
But, decorated in different coloured hats,
Offers a few words like a wound-up gramophone

When she is gone, mouths will run
The country will flap like a loose blind
Rattling on into the unknown future

"This prescient poem came from a sense of wishing to hold onto the kind of stability and continuity that the Queen gave us over her seventy year reign, yet with the knowledge that for better or worse, change will always come."

~

ABOUT CLARE:
Clare started writing poetry in 2021, as the country was beginning to recover from the devastation of COVID-19. During the pandemic, she left her job of eighteen years to support her son when he struggled during the lockdown, and who was subsequently diagnosed with Autistic Spectrum Disorder. In the midst of this difficult time, the change in the pace of life enabled her to discover poetry for the first time, and her work has since appeared in various magazines and has been recognised in competitions.
Twitter: @Clare_Starling

Zoran Hercigonja
(CROATIA)

THE MOTHER AND THE QUEEN

From the window of my universe
You wake me up with a spirited smile
which flickers restlessly.
Always upright in everything
those troubled times
You showed me that the scepter
and the crown are not only
richly arranged pieces of power,
already a sacrifice, care and concern
for the people and the nation.
I look to you worldly queen and mother,
the only star with a smile and feeling.
You are collected all my pains,
joys, fears, wanderings,
the hopes of the little man with whom you share
great obligation, kingdom, power.
I saw You worried with a living heart and dream
as rarely as anyone, my queen.
There is no fear in fog, midnight and darkness
with your stalwart heart.
In spite of myself and others
I dare to exclaim:
Long Live The Queen

"Like no other monarch in the history of the world, as a long-lived and great ruler she alone most courageously showed her fragility and human side. Approachable but restrained, she was the embodiment of moral excellence and the strength with which she inspired the people around her."

~

ABOUT ZORAN:
Zoran is the author of several collections of poetry, short stories and short novels. He works as a professor of computer science, founder and editor-in-chief of several author's magazines, and publishes on a large number of portals.
E: zoran.hercigonja@gmail.com
W: hwww.zoran-hercigonja.webnode.hr

Rohan Facey
(JAMAICA)

THE FINAL WAVE

From the steps of the
darkened carriage –
She turned, waved –
one last time

The roses bowed
Candles flickered
and the rivers pushed against
a leaden sky

Then – the world held sway
to sudden silence

Flags half-mast.
Global bells tolled
and
England wept today.

End of an era – History wags
its tongue.
Time spells out Her Majesty's
grace, dignity, decency.

Perhaps history will
never tell of a kinder soul.

"I wrote this poem because I admire the Queen for her 70 years of unswerving reign and service to Britain, the Commonwealth and the world. She personifies grace, rectitude, devotion and unmatched leadership."

~

ABOUT ROHAN:
Rohan is a multiple award-winning contemporary poet. He mainly writes about human relationships and things that affect us universally, and his poems have appeared in local newspapers, books and international anthologies.
E: PoeticFirerf@yahoo.com

Kathryn Sadakierski
(Massachusetts, USA)

QUEEN OF HEARTS

She may have reigned seven decades,
But the mark she's made
Will persist much longer than this,
Her memory remaining
In the hearts of nations
Around the globe,
The world placed on her shoulders
When only in her twenties
Holding the orb and sceptre,
Bearing up her own grief,
The loss of her father, the king,
She took up the mantle,
Head held high, no tears,
Only pride
To serve the people,
Vowing to do her duty
In the face of all odds.

With us through war,
Wide-ranging change,
Pandemics and pain,
She was a constant source of strength.
It was never just about corgis and tea parties,
Her wardrobe's whimsical pastel shades
Belying the fierceness of her resolve,
Determination, dignity,
A brave face embodying regal grace.

The years rolled by like the royal carriage
Down the streets filled with well-wishers,
Not merely fans, but those who sincerely felt
Connected to this benevolent presence
Presiding over the commonwealth
Like a grandmother to us all.

So we find ourselves now,
Here to continue
Meeting the day, unafraid
To crown this life
In a hopeful light,

The faith that we, too
Can lead the way
On to a better place
Where the song of Her Majesty
Will forever resonate.

"Amazed by the universal impact the Queen had, including such a strong following in the United States, I was drawn to write about the legacy of the iconic monarch. As an avid reader of British history (naturally, focusing on the royals!), I was compelled to reflect on the Queen's inspiring balance of grandmotherly gentleness, steadfast fortitude, preservation of tradition, and leadership through transformative times."

~

ABOUT KATHRYN:
Kathryn is a poet whose work has appeared in journals, literary magazines, newspapers, and anthologies around the world, including: *Capsule Stories, Ephemeral Elegies, Halfway Down the Stairs, Hedge Apple, Loyalhanna Review, Mediterranean Poetry, October Hill Magazine, Songs of Eretz Poetry Review, The Avalon Literary Review, The Bangor Literary Journal, The Orchards Poetry Journal, The Voices Project, Toyon Literary Magazine, Visual Verse: An Anthology of Art and Words, Voices de la Luna*, and *Yellow Arrow Journal*. She holds a B.A. and M.S. from Bay Path University in Longmeadow, Massachusetts.
E: sadski7@gmail.com

Catherine Nicolson
(ENGLAND / NIGERIA)

A WOMAN OF STANDING

She was known for her blue, blue eyes
and her pearly pink and white complexion.
She never followed the latest trends
but always wore hats with minimal brims,
and the very brightest of primary colours,
in order to stand out bold in the crowd:
to be seen to be seen.

In the last year she could only stand
with a stick, but still she supported,
turned up on time, stepped and smiled,
shook waiting hands, listened to speeches,
appeared with the rest on the balcony
to watch the Red Arrows fly by once again,
interminably fast.

She loved horses and dogs, headscarves
and brooches, recalcitrant children.
It was said that she'd tired
of church services and fresh paint's
implacable though honourable intentions.
But of her husband, two paces behind her,
she never once tired.

After he died she shrank in stature,
except for her smile which stayed the same.
'Mobility issues' meant small black shoes
held feet worn out by a lifetime's standing.
If anyone happens to wonder what
in the world she was good for, it would be
all of us that she stood for.

*"The poem is written to celebrate the Queen's steady presence
throughout her own - and the nation's - life. It began, as so often,
with a couple of phrases which haunted me in the middle of the
night, when I was trying to pin down the source of the Queen's
mysterious yet all-embracing influence on the country's sense of
identity. Having spent much of my own time abroad, or in very
different areas of Britain, I felt that the Queen's consistency yet*

open-mindedness about the rest of the world, through which she too travelled widely and during periods of great change, was a remarkable achievement."

~

ABOUT CATHERINE:
Born in Nigeria, now living in London, writer and poet Catherine has worked as a stills photographer, costume designer and film-maker.
E: cmparmenter@gmail.com

Grace Matson
(Wisconsin, USA)

YOUR MAJESTY YOU HAVE GONE HOME

Your Majesty, you will be sorely missed.
Your country, and the world are on that list.
Seventy years on the throne.
You have finally gone home.
Now without you, how can we all exist?

"Queen Elizabeth II has had a place in my heart ever since my oldest sister moved to England in 1978. Following the Queen and her family has been an interest for me and my sister ever since. Queen Elizabeth II will continue to be in our memory."

~

ABOUT GRACE:
Grace has written and published poetry for over five years. She has been published in *Voice of the River Valley* and *The Blue Heroin Review*, as well as a number of community newspapers in Wisconsin. It is Grace's hope that she both entertains and evokes emotion with her poetry.
E: @Matsong61@gmail.com

Pravat Kumar Padhy
(INDIA)

THE PORTRAIT

With her tender touch
She caresses all
As the silhouette of flying birds
In the azure sky
Kisses to the morning sun
Scripting poetry of freedom.

Like a tree
She spreads branches
Of love and care
And the blossoms of good wishes
Carry the fragrance
Far and near.

She muses in silence
With her crescent smiles
As stars of brilliance
Gently gaze through her eyes.

Under the calmness of the moon
The rising lyrics of waves
Rhymes the longshore of fulfilment
And she dwells in her dream
With the boundless time.

"This poem is dedicated in memory of the great woman of the century, and her service to mankind."

~

ABOUT PRAVAT:
Pravat is an award-winning Indian/English poet, haikuist, and essayist. He has a Master of Science and Technology, and a Ph.D from Indian Institute of Technology. His Japanese short form of poetry has been widely published and anthologized, his tanka is included in *Kudo Resource Guide*, University of California. He has also published seven collections.
Blog: www.pkpadhyblogspot.com
FB: @pravat.k.padhy

Vanessa Caraveo
(Texas, USA)

FOR ELIZABETH II

Quietly, she embodied evolution.
Initially seen as a fairytale queen,
young and beautiful as roses in bloom,
but later in life a star to orbit,
an immovable piece of each family.

She was the kind and motherly smile
who held nations together with her grace,
delicately passing through the eras,
her splendid character unfazed,
patient and pure as can ever be.

To have ruled longer than anyone else
and left none offended in her wake,
only in awe of her sense of duty.
She did not take nor covet in life,
living only for heartfelt moments.

A picture of acceptance and faith.
A portrait of what a person can be
if they can abstain from casting blame.
A breathing symbol of humble kindness.
All this and more was the English queen.

Events that may have shaken another,
causing them to shatter and weep
passed her by with scarcely a scratch,
such was the strength of only she.
She will be grieved for decades more
even as she watches us, patiently.

One must wonder, or perhaps assume
that surely she wears the whitest wings.
Who else but her could fill them out,
with years upon years of memories?
She was charity, respect, and love.
Long live the soul of the English queen.

"Elizabeth II's immense grace, sense of duty, and devotion to a life of

service inspired me to write this poem in order to highlight all her incredible qualities she possessed, and the exemplary leadership she displayed throughout her life."

~

ABOUT VANESSA:
Vanessa is an award-winning author, published poet, and artist. She is involved with various organizations that assist children and adults with disabilities, and enjoys working with non-profit groups and volunteering in the promotion of literacy. Vanessa has received international recognition and awards for her literary work, and has been published in *Literature Today Journal, Poetrybay, The Raven Review, Anacua Literary Arts Review, Latinidad Magazine, Voices de la Luna Literature* and *Arts Magazine*, and in various anthologies.
E: vanec2485@hotmail.com

Dr. Ana Stjelja
(SERBIA)

THE MAGNIFICENT QUEEN

You carried a heavy burden
Since the young age.
You, Elizabeth Alexandra Mary,
So devoted and so dignified woman
Whose reign was a magnificent one
And will be written down
In golden letters in the book of world history.

Only you could smile in the hardest times
To give comfort to your nation.
As only you could wear bright coloured dresses
And flowery hats
And still look so beautiful, so elegant
Even in the old age.

You were a fashion icon, a role model
The source of all female virtues.
Serious when necessary
Funny spontaneously
The proof that women are so powerful
And capable to be true leaders.

Your long impressive life was
Like a novel or a movie
So inspirational and exciting.

Your fame will never fade away
You will always be remembered
As The Queen.

"I have always been fascinated with the Queen Elizabeth's magnificent reign, her personality and her devotion to her duty, and I always considered her the most stylish woman in the world. She was an icon, a symbol of one era, a woman who is capable to rule and be a mother figure, not just for her own children, but for the whole nation. Despite of the burden she carried, and the big responsibility she had, she remained strong and righteous, faithful and loyal to the tradition. She is one of a kind, she marked one era and that is so fascinating and inspirational."

~

ABOUT ANA:
Ana obtained her Ph.D on the life and work of the Serbian woman writer Jelena J. Dimitrijević. She is a poet, writer, translator, journalist, researcher and editor, and has published more than 30 books of different literary genres. Ana is also the Editor-in-chief of the *Alia Mundi* magazine for cultural diversity, online literary magazine *Enheduana,* and *Poetryzine,* an online magazine for poetry in English. She is a member of the Association of Writers of Serbia, the Association of Literary Translators of Serbia, the Association of Journalists of Serbia and the International Federation of Journalists (IFJ).
W: www.anastjelja.wixsite.com/anastjelja
FB: @ana.stjelja1
FB: @stjelja.ana
Instagram: @ana_stjelja
LinkedIn: @ana-stjelja-b933491a0

Masudul Hoq
(BANGLADESH)

ELIZABETH

We have queens in fairy tales;
Suyorani Duyorani

Suorani goes into exile
Only Duyorani survives

But I never met
with them

Actually the real queen
You were Elizabeth!

In my eyes
All the queens of the world,
You are the best - you are beyond all wars

Somewhere in Buckingham Palace
There is no lack of light;

But everything except you
a feel without light!

"Her personality and lifestyle inspired me. Her philosophy on anti-war inspired me, especially her thoughts on peace. And the contribution of Queen Elizabeth made on spreading peace throughout the world was worth praising."

~

ABOUT MASUDUL
Masudul has a Ph.D in Aesthetics and is a Professor of Philosophy at a government college. He is a contemporary Bengali poet, short-story writer, translator and researcher. His previous published work includes short stories *Tamakbari* (1999), *The poems of Dhonimoy Palok* (2000), *Dhadhashil Chaya*, which translated version is *Shadow of Illusion* (2005) and *Jonmandher Swapna* which translated version is *Blind Man's Dream* (2010), translated by Kelly J. Copeland. Masudul also translated T. S. Eliot's poem *Four Quartets* (2012), and Allen Ginsburg's poem *Howl* (2018) from English to Bengali. In the

late 1990s, for three years he worked under a research fellowship at The Bangla Academy. Bangla Academy has published his two research books. His poems have been published in Chinese, Romanian, Mandarin, Azarbaijani, Italian, Russian, Turkish, Nepali and Spanish.

E: masudul.hoq@gmail.com

Michelle Morris
(ENGLAND / SOUTH AFRICA)

THE WORLD HAS LOST A QUEEN

The world has lost a queen
But Heaven has gained an angel
Time marches on, and
Each monarch has their moments

Gone but not forgotten
Forever in our hearts and minds
Now with Philip hand in hand
She lives in Heaven by his side

"The passing of Queen Elizabeth II is a sad loss to her country and the planet. She was a monarch for over 70 years, which is a lifetime of service to her people. We are grateful for her reign. Let's not forget that she was also a woman, mother, grandmother, sister, wife, and leader. It is difficult to deal with the loss of a loved one, but even more so when you share that person with the world. The world has lost a queen. Rest in peace, Queen Elizabeth. Philip is waiting for you."

~

ABOUT MICHELLE:
Michelle is a British and South African writer. She has been writing uplifting, inspiring and thought-provoking poetry all her life, and has been published in a number of poetry anthologies.
Instagram: @michellemorrispoet
Twitter: @MichellePoet

Vyacheslav Konoval
(UKRAINE)

WINDSOR'S GRANDMA

The clatter of hooves from a proud mare,
which pulls the carriage swaying,
lucky lady Queen,
carriage's step of to us lead, she dares.

Look at the carriage!
there is a smiling grandmother in it,
she is wearing a blue hat
her luggage is nearby,
as well as candy packages.

Children run up,
they surround the Queen,
candy is waiting for the little one,
they go to the lawn
stripes lie underfoot,
their colour is green.

Draws a smiling mood,
decorates as a bell,
Liz is rich in heart,
without money, clothes, and food.

*"The Queen was a great friend of Ukraine and, as a symbol of the
unity of the Great Nation, forever entered world history as a person
who took responsibility for the continents and the commonwealth of
states. It is a great honour to be involved in writing a poem for such
a beautiful theme."*

~

ABOUT VYACHESLAV:
Vyacheslav's poems have appeared in many literary journals,
including: *Anarchy Anthology Archive, International, Sparks of
Kaliopa, The Lit, Allegro, Mere Inkling,* and many others. His poems
have also been translated into French, Scottish, and Polish.
E: slavakonoval@gmail.com
FB: @slava.konoval (Slava Konoval)
Instagram: @slava.konoval

Joan Leotta

(North Carolina, USA)

A PRIVATE MOMENT

Watching her nation say goodbye,
witnessing the Windsor's public grieving
I felt one with them, when I
learned her moment above ground
would be hidden from
ever-present cameras.
Internment was only
for the unreserved tears of
family and close friends.
When a child dies suddenly
as ours did,
shattering the anticipated
order of life
hundreds filed into the
funeral home to pay respects
to this kind, smart, handsome
nineteen-year-old.
Hundreds crowded into
the church.
Many shared their sorrow.
However, none but
Family did we invited
to stand with us, to
witness that last moment,
when he was lowered
into the place prepared for him
among soft spring grasses
of the nearby cemetery.
I do not recall if we
tossed flowers on his coffin
as it was lowered,
but I think I stretched out my arms
in an awful empty moment of
physical farewell replacing
actual good-by hugs of
so many simpler partings.
I'm glad the Windsor family
also had that privacy
for that last parting
with their loved one,

one private moment
after hours of support for others
that is public grief.

"I needed to write about the Queen's family and their need for privacy, even with all of the public ceremonies they held, so that the country could grieve. Their generosity extended all the way around the world so we could all share these moments - but they had to keep one moment just for themselves, the actual internment, and I understood because I did the same when our son died. Many hundreds came to his funeral, but I kept the actual interment private."

~

Joan's writings are in E*kphrastic Review, Pinesong, The Sun, Brass Bell, Verse Visual, anti-heroin chic, Gargoyle, Silver Birch, Ovunquesiamo, Verse Virtual, Poetry in Plain Sight, MacQueen's Quinterly, Yellow Mama*, and others. She's a 2021 Pushcart nominee, received Best of Micro Fiction, 2021 (Haunted Waters), nominee for Best of the Net, 2023, and 2022 runner up in Frost Foundation Poetry Competition. Her second chapbook, *Feathers on Stone*, is coming in late 2022 from *Main Street Rag*. She is a member of the North Carolina Poetry Society, a member and area representative for North Carolina Writers Network, and on the stage side of her work, member of, and as the coastal area representative for NC's Tar Heel Tellers and coordinates poetry workshops and readings online through her Brunswick County's Arts Council.
FB: @joanleotta
Twitter: @joanleottawrite

Brendon Feeley
(ENGLAND)

UNTITLED

The longest reign in our history.
A shining light that we'll miss bitterly.
A Queen that reigned with poise and grace.
Our steadfast rock cannot be replaced.
A sadness echoes through the land.
Celebrations of her legacy will be grand.
A tribute to the purest public servant.
The outpouring of emotion will be fervent.
Seven decades in service tells your story.
Humility surrounded by your glory.
Today we mourn the news you've passed.
In respect, we fly the flags at half-mast.

"Queen Elizabeth II is the only monarch I have ever known, and I admire a reign of over 70 years - spanning eight decades - that has seen a tremendous amount of love, loss, and grief, and this is my tribute to a true matriarch of a number generations."

~

ABOUT BRENDON:
After a tragic accident in 1998, Brendon was left paralysed from the chest down and lives as a wheelchair-bound, spinally injured tetraplegic. Brendon lives with mental health issues, including anxiety, depression, and post-traumatic stress disorder, and writes modern and striking poetry that he uses as a therapeutic outlet for his emotions.
W: www.linktr.ee/brendonfeeley
FB: @brendonfeeleyofficial
Instagram: @brendonfeeley

Lidia Chiarelli
(ITALY)

QUEEN ELIZABETH'S ROSE

Your pink rose, Queen Elizabeth,
will continue to grow
in my garden
and its sweet fragrance
will intoxicate my soul
in the wavering light of the sunset.

I want to think of you
"forever young"
smiling and waving to the crowd
- the Union Jack flying high
over Buckingham Palace …

Then as in dream I will hear
your voice again
… words making their way
towards a pearly sky

but lost too soon
in the distant horizon …

"My long career as an English language teacher has led me to speak often about Queen Elizabeth to my students and, over the years, a deep affection for Her Majesty has taken root in my soul. This poem is meant to be a small tribute to the Queen who has become so important in my life."

~

ABOUT LIDIA:
Lidia has six Pushcart Prize nominations, and the Grand Jury Prize at Sahitto International Awards (2021). Her writing has been translated into 30 languages, and published in more than 150 poetry magazines, and on web-sites in many countries.
W: www.lidiachiarelli.jimdofree.com
W: www.lidiachiarelliart.jimdofree.com
W: www.imaginepoesia.jimdofree.com
FB: @immagine.poesia

Bernice Baker
(ENGLAND)

WHETHER IT BE LONG OR SHORT

She did serve us so well
With abundant honour, grace,
And unfaltering resilience despite
The weight of her crown,
Most beautiful to behold but
Heavier than most of us could ever bear,
Yet her lifetime promise,
Made to each of us,
Was surely kept as
She was a lifelong advocate
For all of us
She kept us together,
By being ours
And we were hers, most gladly as
For us, she was a constant, a comfort,
For the joyous moments in life
As well as those marked by sorrow

Now, we will mark this most pivotal moment,
For her,
For us,
By standing together.
We do this not bound by duty,
But to make true our own unspoken promise.
We will now honour her through our own grace,
United in our shared gratitude
For evermore;
For she did serve us so well.

"I was inspired to write a piece inspired by the Queen as an acknowledgement of the fact that so many of us have had the utmost respect for the Queen throughout her reign, whether we are a Royalist or perhaps more ambivalent towards the monarchy."

~

ABOUT BERNICE:
Bernice recently returned to writing after having not written creatively for almost 18 years. She enjoys writing about the

everyday; from the beauty of the mundane to the pressures of modern life. She also likes to explore our connection to nature and nature's influence on mental well-being. She has been featured on *BBCCWR* to discuss her writing, as well as having pieces published by *Wildfire Words, Wee Sparrow Poetry Press, Harness Magazine, The Mothers: Life in Lockdown,* and the *'Spaces and places that changed me'* virtual exhibition.
Instagram: @agirlpoet

Vimala Thanggavilo
(MALAYSIA)

QUEEN IN OUR JOURNEY

Lost precious diamond,
By the royal family,
Not an ordinary bond,
A lifetime spent divinely.

Everyone is mourning her leave,
I'm mesmerized by our iron queen,
Her vibes throughout the journey,
Since the day of crowning.

Majesty began the service,
Strength of fifty over countries,
Being light for many,
Touched everyone's souls,
With sincerity and credibility.

Nationwide known,
The memorable moment we have,
We will console our life,
To live further without an iron queen,
Physically but for sure memorably.

Peace has rosed,
In majesty beautiful smile,
Power of queen grace,
Live lively in heaven

"An honour to present this poem to our beloved Queen as a volunteer from one of the Commonwealth countries. Inspired by Queen's aspiring action on the pure dedication towards all the countries' development equally. An opportunity to exhibit my words for a beautiful soul."

~

ABOUT VIMALA:
Vimala is the daughter of Mr. & Mrs. S. Thanggavilo M. Thevanai. She has co-authored over 50 anthologies, and has had her work published in a number of magazines including: The *Inscribing Hunch, Legends*

Times Africa Magazine and *The Ink Dew Times.*
E: lald_tv@yahoo.com
FB: @Vimala T Thevanai
Instagram: @fun_luv_joy
Instagram: @uninterruptible_quotes

Jonathan Ukah
(ENGLAND / NIGERIA)

A PURPLE REIGN

We show gratitude for your long, purple reign,
Which began at the dewy dawn of your youth,
When teenagers struggled to overcome their rage,
You mounted a throne as though it were a horse.
We were deep asleep when your father sadly died,
And were distraught from the shadows of the storm,
When the earth collapsed on our heavy heads.
You arrived overnight from the Horn of Africa,
No longer the wary daughter of a reigning royal,
But the sensitive steward filled with self-sacrifices,
A smile floating in the air for any fallen face,
The safest haven for the broken-hearted.
When kings rise and fall like sacks from the sky,
Slaughtered in wars, dethroned in pyrrhic peace;
When empires woke from their slumbering sway,
Celebrating anniversaries steeped with blue blood,
When kingdoms fall prey to the flying arrows of time
Which make no distinction in the shattering mirrors of life,
Let us praise the one who fights against the shadows
And winning a battle that former kings have lost.
You ascended the throne like climbing a mountain,
Your ladder is the people on whom you placed your feet;
You did not woo the crown; you wooed the people
And you smeared laughter on their frowning faces.
Though the clouds hung low on the evening sky,
You dispersed the dusk with the crown of the morning.

Sometimes I hear the secret fears of Her Royal Majesty,
Determined to be the dome of resilient love and care,
The strength of the weak, the wealth of the poor,
Stacked away till the day the dark sky will finally fall
To crush the poor and the wealthy amidst their days;
Often the orange colour of the royal crown
Is steeped in the wealth and retinue of the royal state.
Every king and queen ascends to the throne of love
Where blessings flow like black oil from a flaming rig,
And then we know we have found the dangerous light
Though there is darkness in the heart of the world.
We listened to you with our bold ears in the air,
Fluffy and wagging like a curious tail,

But when we knew we had smelt the scent of light,
We waited for the day when we would be blessed.
There is glory in the ascension of Grace,
When holier kings suffer from a lack of longevity;
Not by might, nor by our sheer exercise of will
Must our life be stretched beyond the general run?
Therefore, we have come to wave our bleeding hands
Sliced by the same knife that tilted away your life,
And wishing you a safe departure and a safer arrival
To the bosom of the Lord, the tireless throne of Grace.

"I have read and seen so much of the work ethics of the late Queen. Her humility and service to her country is in such a stark contrast to the arrogance and brutality of other monarchs in other kingdoms and nations. This was responsible for her longevity, peace and stability. Stability makes leaders live longer. This is my inspiration for this poem."

~

ABOUT JONATHAN:
Jonathan is a graduate of English from the University of Nigeria. He studied Law in Germany, but lives and writes in London.
E: johnking1502@gmail.com

Joan Mazza
(Virginia, USA)

SECRET LIFE OF A QUEEN

Imagine the same job for seventy-one years,
unable to drive off on your own on a whim,
without a destination or bodyguard. Imagine
everything you do is scrutinized and judged—
or worse, proscribed and orchestrated, no room
for your personal flair or foolishness. Surely,

she must have had days when she wanted to sleep
or read a trashy novel, watch movies in bed
without servants barging in to help her put on
her nightgown. What were her guilty pleasures?
What were her opinions of 45 and family, who
must have seemed like unsocialized toddlers,

ignorant of history and human nature? Did
she ever know the pleasure of making art
or playing a musical instrument? At least
she had her horses, dogs. Wouldn't you bet
there were days when she didn't want to dress in
those heavy pearls and diamonds, or wear a hat

that matched her outfit? Did she recommend
dismissals or get close to those who touched
her, helped her bathe in her old age? Did she
wear sweats? Eat sweets? Let one corgi sleep
on her bed, especially after Philip's final exit?
Did she ever learn the tender art of listening?

Where is the diary where she wrote the candid,
raw truth of what she felt and thought, words
she never whispered or said in public? I want
to know what she thought of Princess Diana
before the scandal and after, what she said
when she heard the news of the crash.

I would like a glimpse at her inner, private life,
the part of herself she kept wrapped in silk
inside a locked cedar trunk, its key hidden
only she knew where, that boisterous,
rebellious self, impatient, witty, irreverent,

yet to be discovered in her private script.

"I have often thought about the life of the Royals and how difficult it must be for them to keep up the image of having it all together and appearing calm, when they are only human. In the wake of the Queen's death, I wonder about all the human details we don't know about her, which prompted my writing this poem."

~

ABOUT JOAN:
Joan worked as a microbiologist and psychotherapist, and taught workshops on understanding dreams and nightmares. She has had over 650 poems published including: *The Comstock Review, Crab Orchard Review, Prairie Schooner, Adanna Literary Journal, Slant, Poet Lore, The Nation*, and in many other publications. She is the author of six self-help psychology books including *Dreaming Your Real Self* (Penguin/Putnam), and is currently working on a novel.
FB: @joanmazza
Twitterr: @joancmazza

John Notley
(ENGLAND / THAILAND)

THE QUEEN OF HEARTS

For seventy years through turbulent and troubled times
one constant has remained.
Thrust to serve us at the early age of twenty-five
the young Elizabeth was Queen proclaimed.
Queen of our country and commonwealth she undertook
Her task and served us well.
Now she is gone and will be sorely missed.
Can she ever be replaced, who can tell?
During times of war together with her parents when
they stayed with us, steadfast
while bombs rained down and death was close.
She was with us to the last
Through all the years that followed
Her consort by her side
she served her people faithfully and gave them
cause for pride.
Her task now done she leaves her realm and as
she from the Abbey departs
the tearful crowd and I will say goodbye to
our own Queen of Hearts.

"I feel fortunate to have lived my whole life under the reign of the late Queen, and join the nation in mourning their sad loss."

~

ABOUT JOHN:
John is a retired travel agent, spending his time between Thailand and the UK. His spare time enables him to write poetry and short stories, some of which have been published.
E: john.notley@gmail.com

Aishwariya Laxmi
(INDIA)

ENGLISH ROSE

"All hail the Queen!"
Are words we've read in books
And seen in films
But Her Majesty Queen Elizabeth II
Was the real reigning monarch
For about 70 years
She visited India thrice
And my dad caught a glimpse of her
When she came to Chennai in 1961
It was near Madras University
And he noted she was young then and
Referred to her as "English Rose"
My generation though
Hasn't had the honour
Of seeing Her Majesty
And now she has passed on
But her legacy lives on
My dad also told me an anecdote
About Her Majesty, the Queen
Apparently, she was on the lawn and
Had a visitor
Who knew not about her royal crown
He mistook her for a regular lady
And spoke to her with great camaraderie
And even posed for a selfie
'Coz he found her a "nice lady"
It's stories such as this
That reveal a person's nature
Surely, she will be missed
Sorely by her country

"As someone who loves the English language, I thought it fit to pen a few lines for the Queen based on my dad's anecdotes and memories of his encounter with Her Majesty."

~

ABOUT AISHWARIYA:
Aishwariya is a writer, editor, blogger, and poet, and holds a master's

degree in communication. She has written and edited for greeting card companies, e-learning companies, MNCs, start-ups, newspapers and advertising agencies. Her poems appear in *Spillwords, The Drabble*, anthologies by Sweetycat Press, Writefluence, Soul Poet Society, ThirdEyeButterflyPress, Indie Blu(e) Publishing, and featured in *Who's Who of Emerging Writers 2021* by Sweetycat Press. She was one of the Top 3 winners of 'High-5: The Great Poetry Hunt Contest' organized by WriteFluence. She has also written flash fiction and essays.

E: mymewse@gmail.com
W: www.aishwariyalaxmi.com
Blog: www.ash.fambase.com

Dr. Ivana Knezevic

(SWITZERLAND / SERBIA)

WELCOME TO DREAMLAND

Goodbye Lady of the Throne!
It's time to fly where You belong.
All blessings and sins
hidden in your smile
will remain a secret for a while.

Your soul is now free
to love, pray and dream,
 to let Your feelings singing
in the valleys where imagination
is bringing
You and Your beloved ones,
right now
is Your chance
for once
to enjoy love at the first glance.

A prisoner of Your life
tightened with the crown,
disciplined to obey the rules,
You are becoming a bird
falling in love with a freedom
of blue sky
where the peace is offered
by angels singing a lullaby.

London will never be the same
but I'll come again to pray
for You
and to listen stories
of Your new life
while writing another poem
for You.

I feel sorry
for You
for missing the liberty of anonymous,
for being told what to do
and for sacrificing a Woman
in You.

Goodbye unforgettable Queen of England!
Good morning, Soul of Dreamland!

"London was the most frequent destination for me when travelling, and the Queen was always around as one of the most powerful and interesting women in history. This poem was written to pay my respects to the Queen, and to wish her peace in heaven."

~

ABOUT IVANA:
Ivana is a medical doctor, specialist in Medical Microbiology and Parasitology, and a poet. She received her MD from the University of Novi Sad, her Ph.D in Medicine (Virology) from the University of Belgrade, and has spent 22 years working in Geneva in the area of standardization; scientific and regulatory overview of biological products for prevention and treatment of diseases. She has published four books in Serbian titled: *Braids of dreams, A secret of hourglass, Blueness in the eyes* and *Down of my soul.*
FB: ivana.knezevic.146
Linkedin: @ivana-knezevic-077ab176

Ernesto P. Santiago
(GREECE / PHILIPPINES)

HARK BACK TO THE GOOD OLD SCENTS OF OUR YOUTH

Just be sure, be sure you do not serve
the sensation of my hunger for the same meal everyday.
My hunger is like a handwritten letter
that lies hidden in a glass vault
and can only be opened by the chosen one.
I am not sure too what would have happened if you served
the wrong meal, intentionally or not.
As a tea connoisseur longing for the taste of care,
so much so, I always check that I myself
dearly long for your lips as hot as boiling water
and as red as summer strawberries.
Indeed I love you juicy like strawberries,
especially when you are in season with my heart.
I am just Elizabeth, I thought; yet a Queen
being a queen, and like any other word whisperer I know
I sit down on my own, only and only for my own,
but in gladness of saints I will let you come
and join me, only if you can keep calm and carry on
my little me time, my sacred place.
Know wherever I am in the world of this world
I am sacredly solid for tea, Earl Grey tea,
made in a teapot by the longing hand
filled with praise wrapped passionately around
the shoulders of peace that I rejoice.
A love am I not, for you, or something of the kind
that will be forever, promised in time?
If as the tea noon I ever share clashes of dreams
with you, O' My Kingdom, silenced too soon,
to death breathe fondly and live again
and hark back to the good old scents of our youth.

"This poem shows my respect and admiration for Queen Elizabeth II's devotion, not only to her people, but also to the World, of which we all part of. My tribute poem is inspired by the Queen's love for tea and her hidden letter."

~

ABOUT ERNESTO:

Ernesto has authored seven books of poetry: *Ang Tinig Ng Ligaw Na Tula / The Voice Of The Wild Verse* - Naji Naaman's Literary Prize Winner 2021. He has also won a number of international poetry awards including; Premio Mundial A La Excelencia Humanistica 'César Vallejo' 2022 from the international literary organization Unión Hispanomundial de Escritores, and Naji Naaman Literary Prize 2021 from Naji Naaman's Foundation for Gratis Culture, Maison Naaman pour la Culture.

E: otsenrepogaitnas@gmail.com

FB: @Ernesto Santiago

Twitter: @otsenreogaitnas

Binod Dawadi
(NEPAL)

THE QUEEN'S LIFE AND HER MEMORIAL WORKS

Queen Elizabeth II ruled in British Monarch,
For 70 years,
She was very much good Queen,
She worked as a queen,
In many states at that time,
She was the longest ruler,
In the history,
She was the greatest performance of artists.

She did many social changes,
She had done more than 600 charities,
She helped military also,
She focused and develop dance, music,
Theatre and films,
She developed modern art,
So she developed the literature so much,
So she is immortal.

"Queen Elizabeth II was very much good Queen who does good work, and wins the hearts of the people and the world. She is immortal and for her praising and her memories this poem is written."

~

ABOUT BINOD:
Binod lives in Kathmandu. He has completed his Master's Degree, majoring in English. His poetry and stories can be seen in a large number of publications worldwide.
E: vinoddawadi9@gmail.com

Lynette G. Esposito
(New Jersey, USA)

THE QUEEN AT BUCKINGHAM

One doesn't define a working woman as a queen
but Elizabeth II, Her Majesty, defined work.

She may not have washed dishes as we do,
but she raised children, grandchildren, ran a household and a country,
did massive piles of paperwork, planned parties, entertained dignitaries,
took part in charities, shared tea, made big decisions, made small decisions—
the list is endless.

It is said a woman's work is never done.
She gave seventy years.
The rainbow over her land is now full circle.

Your Majesty,
you may rest now.
You have set a fine example.
Others will carry on.

"The inspiration for this poem came from the duty and work ethic Queen Elizabeth II showed in her daily life. She, at a young age, pledged herself to serve her country. She kept her word, and I admire her for that."

~

ABOUT LYNETTE:
Lynette has an MA from Rutgers. She has been published in *Readers Digest, Poetry Quarterly, The Philadelphia Inquirer, North of Oxford* and others.
E: nichecom1@aol.com

Sandy Phillips
(ENGLAND)

OUR QUEEN

I stood on a wall and waved to the princess when I was young.
She smiled, in that same way she smiled all her life,
and waved, as she passed by in an open top car.
She too was young, with a whole life to live ahead of her.

When she became Queen Elizabeth, I watched the ceremony on a
very small screen In our neighbour's house, along with many other
people.
Along came Charles, a king in the making, and I loved looking at
Pictures of them in magazines, papers and in the cinema.

When the Queen was expecting Prince Andrew, I was expecting my
Second baby. I thought if she has a boy, then so will I; and I did.
I continued to watch the Royal family with interest. I admired her
Calm, and smiling approach to all her duties and her stamina.

As we both grew older, I thought that betwixt her family and her
duties, she did not have an easy time. But her grace and dignity
always held her high in the public's eye, here and around the world.
I watched as she grew frail, but never thinking of her leaving us.

Now she has gone for her well-deserved rest. Although the nation
grieves,
Indeed, people around the world and her family mourns, all must
look
To the future. We have a new King who, hopefully, will follow the
great
Example he has personally witnessed. The Queen is dead. Long live
the King.

*"I have been watching the Royal family for eighty years. My
memories of her and her father, mother and sister, also of her
children. The way she has conducted her life when she was not at all
expected to become a queen. I admire her for her strength and will-
power to keep up royal protocol. Best of all, that lovely smile she
radiated."*

~

ABOUT SANDY:

Sandy has written stories and poems since the the age of just six, and has had many poems published in anthologies. She has written a book about psychic happenings throughout her life titled: *The Narrow Doorway,* and a children's story published in a book of stories and poems. She has also written articles for psychic magazines, and had a sculpture in the Royal Academy's Summer Exhibition.

E: sandy.phillips72@yahoo.co.uk

Amrita Valan
(INDIA)

QUEEN

Grey clouds chase blue skies
Upon Scottish fields of green
Beloved, your people, gather
To bid adieu, O dear queen.

The slow ringing out
Of your lengthy reign,
Timbres muffled, sad and grave
From whitewashed church steeples,
Toll echoes from their hollow naves
Raise we broken hearts and moistened eyes
To heavenly blue pearl clouded skies.

Alas! Now raised must be, new king, your eldest son
Crowned, must shine a new regent, upon Windsor throne
Sanctified and anointed by laws of provenance divine.

Queen, sleep well, though in our hearts,
Lie heavy epitaphs, which we carry to our graves.
Accept these muted cheers, as final lullabies,
Saddest songs of fond regret.

Goodbye Queen.

Elizabeth Regina, the Second,
Longest serving queen on earth.
Icon of peace, stability, and integrity
Grace and a simple heart.
The harmony of your constancy,
Was beauty of the highest league,
You held together a tiny island,
From the turmoil of modernity.

Like the first Elizabeth, of another golden clime
Benevolent monarch, stately and dignified,
You were gracious, in tumultuous conflicting times
With an always charming sunny smile.
Epitome of sanity, decency and strength
True to your pledge of service, O Queen.

Now rest in peace with Prince Consort Philip,
Queen Mother, your father and sister,
We shall remember your reign,
Solitaire of dazzling splendour,

Sunflower of our mundane earthly days.
Duty well done upon Earth,
Now unite with your family,
Queen, in Heaven's grace.

"I have watched her as a reigning monarch from almost the time I could understand the meaning of the word King or Queen. I liked that she made no waves, was born to high power yet she neither became all about pomp and majesty, nor did she allow herself to forget the dignity of her station. So I am actually commemorating not just her, but the passage of an age of grace, sanity and temperance in all things. Human emotions are almost inexplicable; such as why tears welled up in my eyes when her hearse passed by, or why I stood up each time to recite the Pater Noster with the congregation during the televised funeral proceedings. It deeply affected me, and my gut instinct says it always will."

~

ABOUT AMRITA:
Amrita published has published two books: *Arrivederci Fifty Poems*, (Gloomy Seahorse Press 2021), and *In Between Pauses* (ImpSpired Press, 2021). She has written for numerous national and international online journals and anthologies, and won a jury award for her ekphrastic on Van Gogh's Café Terrace from the Friendswood Ekphrastic Poetry contest in 2021. She was selected to read her poems for the Friendswood Ekphrastic Poetry contest 2022, and has narrated a few short stories for Alan Johnson's Storyboard.
E: amritavalan@gmail.com
FB: @amritavalan

Veronica Roma Pingol
(PHILIPPINES)

BRIGHTEST QUEEN

You're smile make our days bright
brightness that lead us to hope and be inspired
Inspire us to the passion that we love
Love for humanity and world to keep.

Keep the faith intact by your glory
Glory that God given to you
You as the Queen of all Women
Women who showed strength and wisdom.

Wisdom for the benefits of many
Many trials faced even agonies
Agonies, sorrow or pains
Pains that make you the better lady.

Lady of all women that's how we looked you up
Up in the sky with glowing eyes
Eyes that can see your truthfulness and genuineness
Genuineness of heart and soul for everybody.

"This poem is my gratitude to the Queen and a way of showing my sympathy for the family loss, and for the world ..."

~

ABOUT VERONICA:
Currently working in Hong Kong as domestic helper serving a Chinese family, Veronica has recently published her book *Nightbutterfly*.
FB: @nightbutterfly25

Diana Wickes

(Washington State, USA)

THE QUEEN

I have a lengthy connection
with Queen Elizabeth.
My mother who started life
as a British subject,
nurtured a love/hate relationship with the monarchy,
critically watching the abdication of
King Edward VIII, the succession of King George.

When her father became king
I was very young.
I played with Princess Elizabeth
paper dolls. She was my playmate.

On the night of her coronation,
my husband awakened us at two AM
to pay homage to a historic moment,
by shishing short wave radio we caught
her coronation.

The Queen's voice was British,
upper-class, slightly squeaky.
Her messages over the years
seldom held profound content,
reassuring her flock,
"Everything will be Okay."

We were contemporaries:
watching history unfold,
married the same year,
cherishing mates,
raising children,
adoring grandchildren,
surviving changing times.

With deep sorrow, I cry:
"The Queen is dead,
Long Live the King."

"While in England, I took my children to see the changing of the

guard at Buckingham Palace, and was thrilled by the doll house at Windsor Castle. With the passing of Queen Elizabeth, I felt a need to write about my long connection with the Queen."

~

ABOUT DIANA:
Ninety-two year old Diana has been writing since her retirement in 1996. She has published two biographies, two books of poetry, and is a participant in several writer's groups and a Zoom poetry group.
E: dcwix@comcast.net

Anna Ferriero
(ITALY)

THE ANCIENT ELOQUENCE

In the heart of a castle
far from every corner
a legend arises
narrated by witches
to pay off a great torment
or find that chosen one.
Hours of walking
among the voices of the rain
and the awakening of a leaf
in full glance
the frame of a memory.
At the magical border
the beginning of my kiss
between cliffs and dreams below
privilege and great virtue!
The most dreamed gift
I kissed him in that instant
in the heart of a castle
where grace of wisdom
give to the brave
love for the homeland
perfume of hope

"I have correspondence with the Royal House since 2017. REGINA Elizabeth II has always appreciated my books and her sweetness is irreplaceable!"

~

ABOUT ANNA:
Anna is an editor at *Literaven.com*, and has had poetry published in *Paper and Pencil, Poetryzine, Azahar poetry magazine, Enheduana Literary Magazine, Yoga Magazine* and many others.
E: annaferriero71@yahoo.it
FB: @apaixonar
Instagram: @apaixonar

Vicky Walker
(ENGLAND)

OUR QUEEN!

"My name is Elizabeth, as my mother also was. I have reigned upon the throne for a 70 long years.

I had a younger sister, who I dearly loved and missed, our childhood was such fun and frolics with our beloved family.

I the eldest sister, lost her alas too soon. I think about her every day and send a prayer her way!

To my loved ones I was Lilibet, as affectionately known at home.
I travelled far, and did so much by land, sea and car.

So many different people, the hands I have shook over the years. The smiles, the sorrows, and celebrations have been a pleasure to share with you, all these years!

Alas now is the time, for me to rest and pass the crown along.
I thank you greatly for sharing all these memories with me.

I leave you as a Mother, Grandmother and Great grandmother too. I now will join my beloved Philip, and my little sister too.

My lost loved ones have been waiting for me.
I bid farewell to all of you splendid people,

from your Royal Majesty!"

"As a child, I have fond memories of the Queen. She was a constant, positive, important figure, and was there, come what may! Moving forward it will be a big change, as it is the unknown for many. However, it was a great honour to be able to contribute one last positive piece to bid farewell to Her Majesty, and I am truly grateful for that!"

~

ABOUT VICKY:
Victoria works on a dementia unit, and has a great love for helping others. She has recently signed a publishing contract for a book she

has written on the subject of poems about life.
E: vic0409@live.co.uk

Shirley Smothers
(USA)

THE QUEEN OF ENGLAND

You were not always liked
you were often misunderstood.
But I know in your heart
You were always very good.

You were trained from
A very young age not
To show emotion.
But to your Family
You showed your devotion.

Being American I truly
Do not understand.
For you see to me
England and the UK are
a foreign land.

You were considered
A figure Head with no
Real power.
But in my eyes
Many rights you
Did empower.

You were regal
You were beautiful
Your devotion to your
Country was indisputable.

"I have admired Queen Elizabeth since I was a little girl, and have wanted to write a poem about her for many years, but felt - not being a Royal Subject – not worthy. I felt the Queen was often harshly misjudged but I empathized with her, and could see in her demeanour she loved her family, she loved her subjects and she devoted her life to keeping her promise. The Queen will live in my heart forever."

~

ABOUT SHIRLEY:
Shirley is an amateur poet. She mostly writes short stories.
E: Smothers@storystar.com

Jason Kirk Bartley
(Ohio, USA)

QUEEN ELIZABETH II'S HOMECOMING

From royalty to royalty,
God has taken you home,
relieved of all your duties,
In Heaven you trade for your other throne.
How God had you as a ruler,
one upon this earth,
Now you bow at the feet of Jesus,
He who has given you your worth.
He's taken you from your kingdom,
to one up in the sky.
One that is eternal.
One you cannot buy.
Your wealth has not went with you,
Your crown upon the head of your heir.
You spoke of your faith while here
on earth,
since absent from your body,
I know you will be there.
Long live the Queen's legacy.

"The Queen finished her race, and she finished it well. She was a great ruler, and now she's on the other side with God. When she passed away, Jesus was there to welcome her home. What a testimony. What a witness; to know the Queen is safe in the arms of Jesus. Her legacy lives on."

~

ABOUT JASON:
Jason is a Christian poet with a Master's degree in leadership and ministry.
E: jaskirk@live.com

Priya Sharma
(INDIA)

THE INHERENT STRENGTH

Today, the Queen's shoes I wore.
A tough soul, to the core.
All weathers it bore.
Polished or bear,
It shone!
Its strings are gold
Thou to hold.
It stinks not, though old.

To the Queen, was such a shoe sold.
Abolish or cherish
The line it toes!
Glide in!
Me a lonely soul
It beholds!
The shoe contains 'the Queen'
It shows!

"The heels of the Queen have ceased to go: 'tak tak tak , tak tak tak, tak tak tak' all through the Palace, with none befitting to wear her shoes, albeit the crown. Over the unabated debate over her brooches, hats, purses, cars and corgis, I stylishly gazed at her heels, and tried gauging her inherent strength".

~

ABOUT PRIYA:
Priya is a graduate in English Literature, a post graduate in Business Management, and a qualified Screenwriter from University of East Anglia. She has widely contributed *Transformative Ideas on Social and Administrative Reforms* to the Global Consultative Series of the Office of the President of India, and The Standing Committee of The Parliament of India. With over twenty years of collective experience in academics and social service, Priya is awarded by the Vice President of India for Educational and Creative Content Writing.
E: priyasharma27091976@gmail.com

Nivedita Karthik
(INDIA)

THE QUEEN

Evening comes for us, a dusky purple afterglow that
Lights up the skies over the entire world for long hours and
Invites us to bask in its glow, your glow, with full
Zeal and fervour, just the way you would have wished, with floral bouquets of neither
Asters nor mums, although you were a mum and grandmum to us all,
But lilies of the valley, just like you held at your coronation
Eons ago yet not very long ago at all. And we
Thrived like the lilies thrived in hills and amid valleys, in woodlands and amid city parks
Happy for you were a part of our past and present and will always be a part of our future.

"I admire the Queen for how strong she was, both as a ruler and as a woman, how well she juggled her personal and professional lives, and how, despite all that she has seen and lived through, she still stayed strong and always smiling. She is an inspiration to many people across generations - including me - and her steadfast and indomitable spirit will forever live on."

~

ABOUT NIVEDITA:
Nivedita is a graduate in Immunology from the University of Oxford, and currently works as a scientific and medical editor/reviewer. She is an accomplished Bharatanatyam dancer and published poet. She also loves writing stories. Her poetry has appeared in *Glomag, The Society of Classical Poets, The Epoch Times, The Bamboo Hut, Eskimopie, The Sequoyah Cherokee River Journal, The Ekphrastic Review,* and *Visual Verse*. Nivedita also regularly contributes to the open mics organized by Rattle Poetry.
E: nivedita5.karthik@gmail.com
W: www. justrandomwithnk.com
YouTube: @JustrandomwithNK

Sarah Law
(ENGLAND)

BREAKING GROUND

Allow us our moments of grief –
of doffing the everyday doldrums, of offering

hours for someone grander than ourselves.
there is no sense to it, you've argued, well –

I say we have more than one sense, and now
both common and uncommon have responded

with this brief gleaming synthesis. Allow
our feet to tread their labyrinth, its twists

and pauses; fellowships of inner faith
and outer gesture. Tested, proven. Say

that mapped-out mourning broke the ground –
and all the churned-up earth received her crown.

"'This poem reflects on our national mourning for the Queen; how it brought us together during an extraordinary ten days of collective grief. Many who queued for hours to pay their last respects discovered not only the depth of their own feelings, but the breadth of a common bond."

~

ABOUT SARAH:
Sarah has published six collections of poetry, the latest, *Therese: Poems*, with Paraclete Press. Her novel, *Sketches from a Sunlit Heaven*, is forthcoming with Wipf and Stock. She edits the online journal *Amethyst Review*.
Twitter @DrSarahLaw

Maliha Hassan
(PAKISTAN)

LONDON BRIDGE IS DOWN

London Bridge is down,
The code went viral in the town.
The Queen will no longer wear the crown.
The attire of people is black or brown.
Saddened is the air all around.
The reign of Queen comes to an end,
Far and near messages being send.
Funeral plan every six months reviewed,
The grandest plan ever to be construed.
Funeral was planned much before time,
Charles, the three, next in the line.
Final touches of funeral were made.
The casket in Westminster Abbey laid.
King Charles will now rise to the throne.
Will work for the people as are his own.
With patience he waited 70 long years,
To any conspiracy he did not lend ears.
People are coming from far and near,
For a last glimpse of their Queen dear.
 Bouquets, flowers and candles do bring,
In the praise of Queen they all do sing.
To pay homage to the royal figure,
To have a glance, a long queue linger.
Alas! Queen of 15 states is gone,
For next ten days all set to mourn.
Lined in the streets all grieved folklore,
In formation here stood the 'Fab Four',
Princess of Wales and Duchess of Sussex.
William and Kate be Prince and Princess.
The Princess of Hearts was in no way less.
Lady Diana from above witnessing the process.
To the royal tune the melodious choir sing,
'God save the Queen,' to 'God save the King.'

"Queen Elizabeth visited my country in 1961; when I was in Standard 3, St Joseph's Convent School, Quetta, Pakistan. The students of our school had lined up on either side of the road to welcome Her Majesty, and we excitedly waved at her as she passed in front of us. I still have vivid memories of the Queen, and developed a fondness for

her, which I cherish to this day."

~

ABOUT MALIHA
Maliha is an educationist. She has a Masters in English Literature and Linguistics, and as been associated with the field of education for about 30 years. Her poems have been published in various international anthologies, and has written a number of books.
E: mlh.hassan@gmail.com

Kate Young
(ENGLAND)

LONDON BRIDGE HAS FALLEN

waves of mourners mirror the curve
of the Thames
as it snakes the edge
the dredge of a river
steeped in time
through streets and parks
the all-seeing Eye
perched on London's skyline
alighting in Westminster Hall

she has fallen

this monarch

this matriarch

this grandmother

this bridge

joining young and old
a diamond set in gold

the veins of this nation are changed
fault lines appear

crackle across ancient stone
and the bones of this land
quake   tremble

"I was deeply moved by the passing of Queen Elizabeth II. This monarch had been a constant, reassuring presence throughout my life. In an art project set by my watercolour tutor, I decided to use the metaphor of a bridge in the poem. The title refers to the code used to signify the Queen's passing. I hopes that the poem evokes a feeling of loss similar to the loss of a great and noble structure. It ends on a note of uncertainty for the future without this stability."

~

ABOUT KATE:

Kate is a semi-retired teacher and has been passionate about poetry since childhood. Kate's poems have appeared in magazines and webzines in Britain and Canada. Her work has also featured in the anthologies *Places of Poetry* and *Write Out Loud*. Her pamphlet, *A Spark in the Darkness,* is published with Hedgehog Press.

Twitter: @Kateyoung12poet

TAK Erzinger
(SWITZERLAND / USA)

MOON RISE
- after Moon House by Clare Best

You arose without a choice
when innocence
was stripped by betrayal.
There was frost in the air

and a father stood unprepared.
Since then, many moons:
children's round faces, spills of duty
history cupped in each crescent

profiles coined and carried in pocket
And then! The shine of your light,
A consistent vast glow-
slowing conquering the world

bringing a sense of place and tradition
when everything else seemed to change,
rising to the occasion
despite blessings and wounds.

Queen, you conjured spirits
from another life and now
your phantom has receded at dusk
casting a shadow on the wall.

"This poem explores the Queen's fate, beginning when the monarchy was thrust upon her father, and follows her through her reign. The analogy used to symbolise the Queen is the moon keeping in mind the goddess Diana. The moon shines on everyone in the world and this imagery is used to capture how her reach was far and wide, spanning generations."

~

ABOUT TAK:
TAK is an award-winning poet and artist with a Colombian background. Her collection *At the Foot of the Mountain* (Floricanto Press, 2021) won the University of Indianapolis Etching Press,

Whirling Prize 2021 for best nature poetry book. It was also a finalist at The International Book Awards 2022, Willow Run Book Awards and Eyelands Book Awards. Her first audio drama *Stella's Constellation* was produced by Alt.Stories and Fake Realities Podcasts (UK).
W: www.takerzinger.wixsite.com/poet
FB: @poetryvagabond
Instagram: @takerzinger
Twitter: @ErzTak

Carol Tahir
(California, USA)

ELIZABETH

A child who was not meant to be Queen
A woman who accepted the Crown
She wore it well. Her sense of duty , her heartbreaks
molded her and her country.
Always a woman first, with many firsts
Always a mother, with a mothers heart
Always a mediator, with thoughtful diplomacy.
Always a counselor, with words of the wise.
Ninety -six years of a life filled with privilege
Ninety-six years of examples and leadership
Forever in the world's heart and mind.

"My mother looked like the Queen; same startling blue eyes, dark wavy hair and petite stature. They were not to far apart in age. Both gracious and beautiful women."

~

ABOUT CAROL:
Carol is a retired cosmetologist who likes to paint, read and write. Her first love is art and she is lost without that creative outlet. In the last few years she has started using words to paint her stories. Several poems have been published in anthologies, journals, blogs and magazines.
E: akittykat_66@yahoo.com

Elisabetta Bagli
(SPAIN / ITALY)

GOD SAVE THE QUEEN!
(To my mum Rita)

You, born not to be Queen,
Said farewell to your father with elegance and dignity,
With your inner strength and discipline you became the Queen,
Crowned, anointed, consecrated and blessed,
That we have all admired,
That woman, mother and grandmother that loved,
Although tradition, duty and protocol,
Often took you away from your loved ones.
One cannot stop the passage of time
We will no longer see you wear the Crown of Saint Edward,
The Ring and the Ermine
You will no longer have the Orb and the Scepter in your hands:
They will be held, in your memory,
With honor and respect by your son Charles.
We have your official and momentous acts, your legacy
For a world in equilibrium,
Your smiles and your sharp anecdotes
That we liked so much remain forever,
Forever you remain with us, Queen Elizabeth II of England.
God Save the Queen!

"I have always liked Queen Elizabeth II and the role she has played in our society. My mother loved her so much that she put me her name in her honor. I could not help writing words of admiration for her now that she is gone, and together with my mum, she is there, instilling positive thoughts and love in us who are still here, on this earth."

~

ABOUT ELISABETTA
Elisabetta is a translator, writer, poet, essayist, columnist, radio correspondent and representative of several Spanish, Italian and international cultural Associations. She is the author of several poetry books, a collection of stories, a children's book, and articles and essays for newspapers and online magazines around the world.
E: elibagli7@gmail.com

Bill Matthews
(CANADA)

QUEEN, FAREWELL

Sorry from the world, for the loss of your Queen.
Most magnificent Lady, the world has ever seen.
I guess being from Canada makes her ours, too.
The Platinum Jubilee, February 6, 2022.
Her Majesty first visited Canada when I was just one,
My Nanny, adhored her, but was with her first grandson.
She became Queen at the young age of 25,
During her reign, the Monarchy really did thrive.
Always a colourful wardrobe she wore,
Waving at the crowds was never a chore.
Well rounded in life was this demure little Queen,
Much pride in her football, Arsenal her team.
More about this Royal, maybe things you didn't know,
Racing pigeons, riding horses and her Corgis on the go.
Donated a jaguar, an elephant to the London zoo
Two giant tortoises, two sloths also hers too.
St. George's Chapel her new resting place.
Forever be humbled, sweet smile on her face.
Humanity was saddened on the 8th of September,
The world's Queen, who we'll always remember.

"If my Nanny had lived longer, I know I would have taken her to see the Queen. She died when I was eleven. The Queen reminded me a lot of my Grandmother."

~

ABOUT BILL:
Bill lives in a small town, north-west of Toronto. He has been writing poetry for over 50 years.
E: sidney.matthews99@gmail.com

Til Kumari Sharma
(NEPAL)

THE MOTHER QUEEN

Known to world as the shining pearl
Being brave woman of human community

Crown of highness in the ruling board
The value of eternal sunshine

Inspiration to all women
Leading quality of Queen Elizabeth Second

Known in world as the time of strength as 70 years
The huge lesson to all ladies to know her ability to rule over.

The shining star in London
The brave queen of woman crown

She is example of bravery
Mother to her people

The huge pearl of her nation
The eternal light in her leading

The beauty of her talent and wisdom
Crown of bravery to be alive for many years

Amazing star of female bravery
Now missing or demise of her physical body

But eternality of crown and work shines in every hearts of people.
The inspiration of moral ethics

The woman bond for all.
Sad to hear her demise.

"This poem about Queen Elizabeth is to show her strong, leading capacity, and how she is inspirational to all women. Her strength teaches all women to be brave like her."

~

ABOUT TIL:
Also known as Pushpa, Til has published over 6000 poems and 180 essays and other literary works, and is currently doing a Ph.D in English Literature from Singhania University, India.
E: authortilkumarisharma@gmail.com

Francisc Edmund Balogh
(ENGLAND / ROMANIA)

HER MAJESTY

Like a white dove,
the world flew on the palm of
the Queen - caressed him,
doves know how to find their way back home,
people often turn to doves for a moment of purity and escape,
her heart was an open window,
a nest where all of us could return
when it is foggy and rainy ...
That day, the day when the Queen herself
ascended as a white dove
watching over us from above,
tears of angels reached the ground
disguised as petals of white flowers!

"Her Majesty, Queen Elisabeth II was our time's most beloved leader, a beautiful person driven by the ideal of grace, simplicity, harmony. She was, in many ways, the guiding light of the world."

~

ABOUT FRANCISC:
Francisc is a Romanian poet, writer and musician. His work has been published in a number of international anthologies, literary e-magazines and magazines including: *Vort Vergessen* (Germany), *Lettres Capitales* (France), *Opa* and *Cultural Reverence* (India), *The World Poetry Tree anthology* (Dubai), and *One Hand Clapping* and *Lothrien Poetry Journal* (UK).
E: franciscbalogh42@gmail.com
FB: @francisc.e.balogh

Liz Grisaru
(New York State, USA)

A VISIT

The Queen of England came to visit me
at my summer house that isn't really mine.
She admired the tall pines in the yard;
she said they were indeed majestic. The kids
quarreled at board games on the porch,
then ran away downhill to the beach.

Later the Queen suggested an aperitif,
her accustomed pause, but because
it was off-season I hadn't much to offer.
She and I went scrounging in cupboards and found
a dusty bottle in doubtful green left behind
by last year's people, a scant third full.
It wasn't good Scotch or even decent gin;
but she said that it would do, game Queen.

Then to find a glass fit for such a guest
I went rummaging again. I rejected
several old jelly jars. I needed clear,
clear glass, unsmudged, that would comprehend
this, its sole purpose. Above my head
one with a polished rim and small enough
for a royal hand. I made the offering and then
someone's elbow jogged the bottle, spilling
a pool of spirits across the tablecloth.
Being Queen, she didn't move to clean it up,
so back to rummaging among unwashed rags
until I spotted clean tea towels in a pile
left behind like last year's liquor.

I folded one as if it were damask made from silk
spun by the Chinese emperor's favorite silkworms
and placed it beside her arm, within easy reach.
As she sipped her drink, I looked outside and saw
the kids now running along the beach.

"I spent some of my formative years in the United Kingdom, long enough to acquire the habit of now and then encountering the Queen in my dreams. This poem grew out of such a dream and mixes

elements of my experiences in the two places; the US and the UK."

~

ABOUT LIZ:
Liz resumed writing poetry in 2020, after a 30-year hiatus raising two young adults during of whom she is very proud.
Twitter: @LGrisaru

G. W. Colkitto
(SCOTLAND)

A THOUGHT ON MORTALITY
(from scenes following the death of Queen Elizabeth II)

every life has its space
length is no measure of the toil
it is the giving not the I
zealous wills such granite quartz
are found and kept the Omega
beyond a final word the nub
each seeker grabs and there
turns it in their tightened fist
holds it proud and high

each life so precious time
lingers on the lips so all
is hope and like Stromboli
zapspalts the sea a blitz
a zing where steam and lava
boil and toss combine superb
enliven renew alive
this is how the heart
how love conquers death

"I felt the poem allowed me to celebrate the life of Queen Elizabeth II, but also to encompass all who contribute to society."

~

ABOUT G.W.:
G. W. Colkitto is an ex- Inspector of Taxes, Chartered Account, and Bookshop owner. He writes both poetry and prose, and has had short stories and poetry published in magazines and anthologies including: *Ink Sweat and Tears, Envoi* and *Poetry Scotland*. Successful in a number of competitions, his commissioned poems are on permanent display in Linwood Johnstone, and Erskine Health Centres. He is on the Scottish Book Trust Live Literature Directory, and has facilitated workshops for NHS Renfrewshire Network Services, Lochwinnoch Arts Festival and Cinnamon Press.
W: www.gwcolkitto.co.uk.
FB: @George Colkitto Writer

Gary Shulman
(New York State, USA)

FAREWELL DEAR ELIZABETH THE QUEEN

Regal reigning grand dame supreme
You now depart the corporeal realm
Your legacy of life so firmly set
Dear beloved Elizabeth the Queen
Honor, faith familial pride
Your passing so many shall mourn
You fought to elevate those in need
So many are left forlorn
Now the world must contemplate
Your legacy of love and grace
We hail to you dear Elizabeth the Queen
Your memory we all embrace

"Longevity alone does not a respected role model make. Queen Elizabeth was raised in a cocoon of royalty yet was compelled to break out of that cocoon and serve with humanity and dignity, and always with love in her heart. There have been countless royal figures in the world through the aeons who viewed themselves as being above those whom they ruled. It was obvious Queen Elizabeth desired to connect with the hearts and souls of those who sought to put her on a more lofty pedestal. I don't think she wanted that pedestal to be her roost, but rather connect in a more humane way with those who will sorely miss her."

~

ABOUT GARY:
Gary (MS. Ed.) has spent a lifetime supporting vulnerable families and children. He began his career working with children with and without disabilities in an inclusive Head Start program in Brooklyn NY. He then transitioned to become the Special Needs and Early Childhood Coordinator for the Brooklyn Children's Museum for 10 years. His passion for advocacy grew as he worked more and more with parents of children with disabilities. For over 24 years he passionately advocated for the needs of these parents as the Social Services and Training Director for Resources for Children with Special Needs, Inc. in NYC.
E: shulman.gary@yahoo.com

Mihaela Băbuşanu
(ROMANIA)

Haiku

Balmoral full moon-
equally bright from window
His Majesty eyes

"I wrote this haiku for the Queen because, for me, it was a symbol of permanence, common sense, discretion, of the female monarch, and of the strong woman of Great Britain."

~

ABOUT MIHAELA:
Mihaela is an internationally published award-winning writer and poet, with a large number of publications to her credit.
E: dragoneasa@yahoo.ca
Blog: www.mihaela-babusanu-amalanci.blogspot.com

Marilyn Peretti

(Illinois, USA)

ALWAYS THERE

I'm 87 and she
was always there—
withstanding bombing
at the Palace in WWII,
which I learned about
in front page headlines,
just learning to read
in Indianapolis.

Living in Chicago
by 1959, on TV
I watched Elizabeth
and Philip arrive
by ship on Lake Michigan,
stepping off at
Buckingham Fountain,
though not her same
Buckingham.

Years later
I did stand outside
Buckingham Palace
and wonder—
wonder what she does
behind those ornate
iron gates, behind
those thick walls

when a servant
brings breakfast
on a perfect tray,
the Dresser brings
her flowered dress,
and someone again
serves 4 pm tea,
precise and sweet
with scones and jam.

In magazines
I read of her Corgis

and her horses—
oh yes! The Queen
was happily off to
the races at every chance,
cheering her horse to win,
or else going riding herself
as on her old black pony,
Fern, at age 96!

*"The Queen herself inspired this poem since she has been in my life
all my many years — as a positive, productive mother and national
leader. She had dignity and sincerity which lifted the spirits and
standards of the world. She was a constant! No matter what else was
going on in the world, this Queen reflected kindness, goodness and
dedication to a job."*

~

ABOUT MARILYN:
Marilyn is member of several poetry writers groups, and has been
active at workshops, readings and critiques for a number of years.
She has attended the Iowa Summer Poetry Festival, and the Galway
Poetry Festival, and is proud to have been published online at *New
Verse News* 14 times. She has also had poems published in journals
including: *Kyoto Journal, Christian Science Monitor, Talking River,
Journal of Modern Poetry, California Quarterly*, and others. Nominated
for the Pushcart Prize, she has self-published two books on cranes:
Let Wings Take You, and *Cranes to Come* - once featured at Int'l
Crane Foundation. Her work is also featured in *Lichen-Poems of
Nature, Angel's Wings, To Remember-To Hope*, and most recently
Poetry for Ukraine and *Behind the Mask*.
W: www.perettipoems.wordpress.com

Javisth Bhugobaun
(MAURITIUS)

THE LATE LIVING LEGEND

An icon as famous as time,
Yet her clock stopped ticking
And the world halted for a minute.
The soul that her body once housed has been left empty.
And the white Palace seemed gloomy.

The one that we all thought immortal
Has come and gone.
A life filled with millions of memories.
A life that fed millions with memories.
Memorable memories.

She once walked the soil I now walk upon.
Visited the capital I now visit too.
Generations saw her, some through their eyes, some through boxes.
She planted the seed that now grows our crop
And gave us our flag that blows among daffodils,
The same daffodils that will carry her songs around the world.

In one hundred years, in a history book,
A child will feel none of the shock
The world felt,
Will see none of the hearts broken,
Will hear none of the rain hitting black umbrellas,
Yet will be inspired. Inspired to be greater like Her Majesty the
Queen.

A late living Legend that our mind will forget,
But our hearts will remember.

*"The Queen was always an icon and important figure to Mauritius as
we were part of the British Empire."*

~

ABOUT JAVISTH:
Javisth is an 18 year-old student of literature. With the help of his
English teacher, his mentor, he learned the ways of poetry and how
to better himself. He was previously published in *Poetry for Ukraine,*

The Pangolin Review and *Contemplations* - about the Wakashio oil spill on the south-east coast of Mauritius.
Instagram: @javisth.b

Keith Jepson
(ENGLAND)

A FINAL JOURNEY

Gone is the second Elizabethan Swan, they never survive their
partners long.
Rainbows pause in castle skies, the Queen of colour they whisper and
sigh ... has gone.
The piper stands beneath a window and plays the final awakenings,
In Crathie Kirk a candle flickers and wisdom, duty, service, honour
are passed seamlessly.
At Arthur's Seat our Lady lies, no more Gillies dance in heathered
sky's.
"Will we not see thee again?"
Our Queen of colours is dead, it is said, heralded in gold, silver and
lead.
Muffled hooves on measured sand, caressed held with precision in an
immaculate hand.
She is our Queen, is the solemn cry, remembered, respected, revered
all must die.
In death, still dutiful, serving under the nations eyes.
Queuing to join a queue, hour upon hours following the quiet
Thames, our own warm reflections in the water.
People snake, a line of tribute for miles and miles ... "it doesn't seem
real through all the smiles".
Westminster Hall, where ages are captured in the stone, seeped in
the words, stories, art, songs, blood and bone. Time stands still and
still we can't believe.
Wreathed in black, flags lowered only once, to gently kiss the floor.
As Autumn enters all our lives and the world is a little darker if only
for a time.
Rest in peace, in memory, monuments and veiled in love.
Monarch. Woman. Human.
We honour you.
Go well.
God Save the King.

*"I wanted to write a poem to celebrate the Queen, and to
commemorate her life and the momentous scenes of her passing and
funeral. She has always been a constant in my entire life, and I
believe her life of service is above the politics of life."*

~

ABOUT KEITH:
Keith has recently published his first poetry collection titled: *A Song of the Severn*. He takes his inspiration from the landscape, people and places of Shropshire, and his global travels.
E: team@maxbikespr.co.uk

Russell Willis
(Vermont, USA)

HER ENGLAND: A CONSTANT RAIN

Witnessed from across the pond
Hers was a gentle rain,
Softening an Earth pounded by
War and troubles
Partisans and disease

A constant, quiet rain,
Nurturing each new season,
Each new spring,
With a soft breeze:
Her whispered laugh and whimsical glance.

Sometimes blanketed by a fog of
Indifference or uncertainty.
Always to emerge
Weathered, yet abiding:
A gentle rain softening a hardened Earth

"Being of English and Scots-Irish lineage, I have always been fascinated by British history, particularly British royalty. That connection was reinforced when my wife Dawn and I were married within a few days of Charles and Diana. Since then we have visited the British Isles several times, each time revelling in royal history. But on another level, as an academic interested in sociology and church history, I have found that Queen Elizabeth II was an extraordinary historical character, brimming with integrity and constancy in an age of political chaos and cultural upheaval. It is this character for whom this poem was composed and is dedicated."

~

ABOUT RUSSELL:
Russell emerged as a poet in 2019 with the publication of three poems in *The Write Launch*. He has published poetry in over thirty online and print journals, and twenty print anthologies.
W: www.REWillisWrites.com
FB: @russell.willis.1217
Instagram: @russell.willis.1217

Alex Chornyj
(CANADA)

LADY OF THE AGES

She was pride and principle
A devout monarch
Commitment to duty
In her lengthy reign,
Longest serving tenure
Was a natural
Never let her stature
Rise above the people.
Was their faithful servant
A woman of consequence
Who put all others
Before her own needs.
Could see early on
What kind of Queen
She'd be known for
One, all could respect.
In her responsibilities
She did not neglect
Her own family
Walked a fine line.
Worthy of the accolades
Were showered with
Each step had purpose
A poise prim and proper.
Her Christmas message
Held words of encouragement
To lift those up
To offer sincerity.
She gave endlessly
Right to the end
Accepting a resignation
Welcoming England's,
Third female Prime Minister
At the stately Balmoral residence
In her was a dignity
By her, those around,
Shone so brightly
Basking in her light
She had want to share
A lady of the ages.

"I wrote this poem because of my English heritage, and the pride I have in the dedication and loyal commitment Queen Elizabeth always showed to her subjects. Queen Elizabeth was the glue that held the royal family together, and the Commonwealth in times of crisis. She was the soothing and calming that brought lucidness to a confusing situation."

~

ABOUT ALEX:
Alex is a reiki master teacher. He has been writing for approximately forty years, and his inspiration is derived through his spirit guides. He has been published in: *The Canadian Federation Of Poetry, Poetry Super Highway, Touch Magazine, Decanto Magazine, Fashion For Collapse Magazine, I Speak Project, Awaken Consciousness Magazine, Earthborne Magazine, Gloom Cupboard Magazine,The Not Magazine, The Tower Journal, White Mountain Publications, 2Sloitudes Magazine,* as well as a host of others. He has also published three poetry books and two children's adventure books.
E: alex.chornyj@ontario.ca

Manju Kanchuli Tiwari
(NEPAL)

ON THE SAD DAY OF QUEEN'S DEPARTURE

Now you have just reached Westminster Abbey
Where you were married
Where you were crowned
The then Queen! You were a bright blossoming sun
Now you are calm in coffin, blooming as wilted moon.

When I saw you in a car in my country
With massive clapping and exciting
My eleven years old small hands hailed you
Mingled in the ocean of those clapping sounds
Now your coffin!? Shocked the world and my mind

You a never political figure
Ever loved and regarded
Like a goddess in our temple
The plants you planted have become trees
Like flying flags of friendship in my land

Bending their foreheads
In complete silence
And their still faces in your loss
So sad!
Moving our human heart

Your monarchy so good for your land
Your hidden physical body in a coffin!
A huge procession knows all
Your duty and commitment, still remembered
Before the unseen huge audience in the Universe

You're a silent force in common wealth
You're a modern role of best regards
Now monks are chanting; lamps are lit in our monastery
People are praying for the peace of your soul
In this historical event, humanity everywhere!

O' Queen! Slumber in deep sleep
Free from domestic affairs
Free from national affairs
My mind is heavy with grief and sorrow

In your loss!

Your long life and diligence
Your service, compassion, honesty and dedication
Your loyalty to the country
You the never vanishing glory of this era
On this earth, forever and ever!

"When Queen Elizabeth II visited Kathmandu in 1961, following the cordial invitation of the then King, Mahendra Bir Bikram Shah, I was a small girl in my early teens. I was waiting to see the Queen with great excitement. She was in a decorated car. People standing by the side of main road welcomed her with huge clapping. After that, I also saw her face in newspapers, and read the news and views about her arrival. She planted trees in our land as a symbol of friendship between the two nations."

~

ABOUT MANJU:
Manju is a clinical psychologist and an eminent writer of poetry, fiction, plays and essays. She has published 18 books, and has delivered poetry presentations worldwide.
E: manjukanchuli@yahoo.com

Dr. Praveen Kumar Anshuman
(INDIA)

QUEEN: AN EMBLEM OF CHARITY

Longest reign of a queen
Ever in the British History,
Support, Cordiality & Perseverance
Are the ones, unfolding her mystery.

An emblem of Charity
A symbol of Compassion,
Whirling round the whole world
To have an excellent execution.

Be it a Royal or a ruffian
Be it a military or a professional,
She kept her eyes unabashed
And her love was just unconditional.

Sharing was her way of life
Commitment was the key she had,
Round the Globe, for her glance
People were always going mad.

Heaven is the only place for her
Bliss was what she got her whole life,
Moving on her path with utter care
Who read Royal as Loyal all her life.

"I am greatly impressed by Queen's many charities she continued doing throughout her whole life."

~

ABOUT PRAVEEM:
Praveen is an English teacher. His areas of interests are Post-British Drama, Indian Classical Literature, and Dalit Studies. He has published 11 books to-date, and has recently composed more than 17,000 shayaris and 2,000 poems in Hindi.
E: dr.pkanshuman@gmail.com

Arun Hariharan
(INDIA)

HER MAJESTY, THE QUEEN

She ascended the throne when the world was in turmoil,
When the British Empire was in flux and on a wane,
Noble in demeanour was she and yet willing to toil.

In her early years, the globe was once again on the boil,
Yet she professed that peace was the only gain,
She ascended the throne when the world was in turmoil.

She hit the ground running as she was cut from the old foil,
Regality she personified, yet so connected to the grain,
Noble in demeanour was she and yet willing to toil.

Many a tough times, many a controversy they tried to embroil,
But Her Majesty bore it with a smile and ne'er professed pain,
She ascended the throne when the world was in turmoil.

Her charity was legendary, human anguish made her roil,
Not just for mankind but for voiceless animals did she campaign,
Noble in demeanour was she and yet willing to toil.

We now bid her goodbye as she's interred in soil,
But generations surely will remember her noble reign,
She ascended the throne when the world was in turmoil,
Noble in demeanour was she and yet willing to toil.

"For me, Queen Elizabeth II always personified quiet dignity, regality and, above all, a person and a woman who has always stood up to tough times and odds with a strong will, strength and a puissant presence. Her long reign and well identifiable face have ensured that generations across geographies will always remember her as The Queen for a long, long time to come."

~

ABOUT ARUN:
Arun is an Indian Army veteran. An avid biker, author, poet, compulsive traveller, photographer and history buff, he's always loved exploring the unexplored. His collection of short stories *A Baker's Dozen - 13 Chilling Indian Tales of Macabre* was published in

October 2021 by Creative Crow Publishers. His poetry and stories have also been published in a number of international anthologies including: *Quarantine Days, I Ain't a Saint, Unspeakable, Open Skies Poetry, Dandelions: Multiverse of Poems, Efflorescence* and in the literary journal *Rhyvers Beat.*
FB: @arun.hariharan.7
Instagram: @arun_author
Twitter: @arukal
Lnkedin: @arun-hariharan-india

Jan Chronister
(Wisconsin, USA)

THE QUEEN IS DEAD

My car radio broadcast the news.
I should have pulled over
instead of crying the rest of the way home.
I didn't want my husband to think
something was wrong.

My mother's side is English,
all tea and biscuits,
Wedgewood bone china,
Blue Willow ware.

My family lived in Ontario
when Princess Elizabeth and Philip
toured Canada in 1951.
High on my father's shoulders
above the thick crowd
at the station, I saw
her regal profile in the train window—
a sight I'll never forget.

Seventy years of rule,
always well-dressed
with a gracious smile
and legendary hats.
A steady ship in stormy times,
the peace she sought
is now hers.

"Even though I was only two years-old at the time. I remember clearly Princess Elizabeth and Philip's visit to Ontario in 1951, as described in my poem."

~

ABOUT JAN:
Jan's work appears in numerous state, regional and national journals and anthologies. She has won awards from Lake Superior Writers, the Tallgrass Writers Guild, Highland Park Poetry, the Wisconsin Fellowship of Poets, and League of Minnesota Poets. Jan's first

chapbook *Target Practice* was published by Parallel Press at the University of Wisconsin in 2009. *Casualties*, a chapbook of Holocaust poems, was published in 2017. She founded *The Thunderbird Review* in 2013. Her full-length collection *Caught between Coasts* was released by Clover Valley Press in 2018 and was recognized as an Outstanding Achievement in Poetry by the Wisconsin Library Association. A third chapbook, *Bird Religion*, was published in 2019. Now retired, Jan continues to teach poetry workshops and plan poetry events.

W: www.bequempublishing.com/authors/authors-c-d/jan-chronister/

Kay Clayton
(ENGLAND)

OUR QUEEN

She taught us all the meaning of duty
whether monarchist, republican or unsure
She pledged to remain true to the oath that she made
throughout her life she was steadfast and sure

She worked hard to fulfil all her duties
though some days she must have wished to be free
She remembered her pledge to her country
of which she was an excellent trustee

She had such a beautiful smile
and made everyone feel that she cared
She had engaged with all of the world leaders
and her knowledge was readily shared

I will miss knowing that she is my Queen
God save the Queen we would all proudly sing
I will mourn the end of an era
but will welcome her son our new King

"Like many people, the death of the Queen had a profound impact on me, and came as a real shock. Although it was to be expected given her age, everyone hoped it would never happen. The death of the Queen reminded me, and many others, that the Queen had devoted her life to her country and her service was outstanding."

~

ABOUT KAY:
Kay has written poetry throughout her life as a way of working through difficulties and, very occasionally, celebrating success. Choosing not to share her work due to insecurities about revealing too much about herself, Kay has had no work published so far, However, she has started to compile all of her work into an anthology titled: *My legacy*.
E: kay_clayton@hotmail.com

Maid Čorbić
(BOSNIA & HERZEGOVINA)

BROKEN HEARTS

She was such a special woman to me.
so charming and dear, sensitive
to help everyone and to stop the war alone
Although she has survived all types of war
One she couldn't overcome though; life.

The world cried when it heard that she was gone.
Britain is in mourning as if it were my country.
for I loved my queen especially
· and I could never forget her eyes on Will

She only stood for peace and justice.
and as I look today, unfortunately, everything has collapsed.
because she no longer has the right to her life
for her words begin to be a trace and ashes
yet she was somebody and something to the whole world.

Everyone had the right to visit her palace.
On the other side of the wall, we only saw
her kindness when she waved at everyone
and let everyone know that she is strong.
although he gave her feelings and more sadness and illness

because she had the desire to live again
For all time, she was the Queen.
We will never forget the breakdown and tears.
because on that day everything disappeared.
died in a moment, and time does not go back.

"This is to express my gratitude for Queen Elizabeth for her amazing words, and what she says and does for world. She was an awesome person."

~

ABOUT MAID:
Twenty-one year old Maid is the editor of the First Virtual Art portal that aims to bring together poets around the world. His work has been published in anthologies and journals in Chile, Spain, Ecuador,

Bosnia and Herzegovina, San Salvador, United Kingdom, Indonesia, India, Croatia and Serbia. He has also published collections titled: *Sea in the palm of your hand, Stories from Isolation,* and *Kosovo Peony.*

E: detrix233@gmail.com
FB: @globechampion
FB : @xcelendge
Instagram: @zaglavlje.official
Twitter: @maky.broo

Rahim Karim
(KYRGYZSTAN)

QUEEN ELIZABETH

What could this death be?
To die once in a hundred years?
Her, rather, this is a wedding,
What "celebrates" the whole wide world.

Not everyone can live that long
To dream of all about such ... and only.
All my life Princess, Queen,
Not everyone is given to live.

God loved her so much
The throne gave her eternal - rock.
Or was an angel of heaven,
What a beautiful result!

What could this death be?
After all, dreaming about such a whole century ...
Her, rather, this is a wedding,
What "celebrates" the whole wide world.

"I never knew the Queen, but respected her very much as the most majestic woman of our planet. The death of Queen Elizabeth greatly shocked me, so I decided to dedicate this poem to her."

~

ABOUT RAHIM:
Author of the national bestseller *Kamila*, Rahim is an Uzbek-Kyrgyz-Russian Soviet poet, writer, publicist and translator. A Graduate of the Maxim Gorky Literature Institute, Moscow, Rahim is a member of a large numbers of national and international literary associates including: the National Union of Writers of the Kyrgyz Republic, the Union of Journalists of the Kyrgyz Republic, and the official representative of the International Federation of Russian-speaking Writers (London-Budapest) in Kyrgyzstan. He has won a large number of literary awards, and his work has been published in over 30 countries around the world.
E: kamron2003@mail.ru
FB:@rahimkarimov1960

Sheryl L. Fuller
(Illinois, USA)

DEVOTION

Right hand for service and duty, handbag on the left
One sovereign solemn beauty, keep calm and sweetly rest
The angels now hold you, sceptre, orb, and crown
The longest of the royal reign is done
Regarded and guarded in life and death
Defender of faith until your last breath
Heart of devotion for generations
Sorrow and unity among royal relations
Alone as you are called to come
Called to one, heavenly home
May you arrive with blessed ease
To honor your devoted days
And may you rest in eternal peace
As the royal piper solemnly plays

"Being a wife, mother, and grandmother is challenging enough, but add to that being the Head of State is a great undertaking. Queen Elizabeth II handled her responsibilities with grace and devotion. She was, and remains, an inspiration."

~

ABOUT SHERYL:
Sheryl is a writer, singer songwriter, and performing artist. Her writing is inspired from her many life experiences and her work has been published in a number of publications including *Poetry For Ukraine.*
E: playnicekids@comcast.net

Hasanul Hoq
(BANGLADESH)

THE UNIVERSAL QUEEN

Emptiness around the palace
No life in the lighting of night
No fragrances of your garden coming to us,
Why the flowers are mourning,
No single evening,
comes with birds sweet chirping,
Fountains have stopped to burst,
You were a great creature of reliance, respect and love.
The Royal chair is still moving
I solely believe, "You are"
We solely believe, "You are".

The generation, used to go to bed
listening Royal tales,
Still they sleep hearing YOU.

When the word 'Queen' comes,
You become visible in our mirror of time,

'Departure' and 'Leave',
Never the same!

"I am writing this poem on Queen Elizabeth because, like most people, I have a soft feeling for her. I am inspired by her responsibilities; it was so tough handling a large kingdom, but the Queen did it with great skill. Her contribution to her people, as well as the world, was remarkable!"

~

ABOUT HASANUL:
Hasanul graduated in English Literature and Language from the Jagannath University, Dhaka. He is involved in writing, translating and editing, and loves to make short documentaries.
E: shoummo1971@gmail.com

Francis Muzofa
(NAMIBIA / ZIMBABWE)

SHE WAS SOUND, NOT LOUD

"When an old woman dies, a library burns to the ground."
When a village loses a grandmother, the village is poorer
The villagers wish they had taken notes
You were not a village grandma
You were not only for England
You were not only for Europe
You were for the world
A World Queen

Your reign transcended boarders
Your reign inspired nations
Your reign inspired the young and the old
The rich and the poor
Your reign was long but you were never short
You were not loud but you were sound
You could have flown but you walked
So you could walk with pedestrians
You had the power and the resources
But you didn't manipulate the system

You defied the odds
The gender card was quashed
The age myth squashed
First they said you were a woman
Then they said you were too young
Later they said you were too old
They never run out blame
Do they

You started early
And finished late
But you were never late
Never a let down
The quality remained
The zeal remained
Humility maintained

A humble servant
You were

"The inspiration behind this poem is the the simplest and humility that the Queen exhibited throughout her reign. It was so humbling to marry her status and her humility. Like a duck, she stayed calm while peddling seriously under the water. She got things done silently. She didn't abuse her enormous power, she remained human and humble until her last day. To that I salute. To that I wrote."

~

ABOUT FRANCIS:
Francis (aka @Pope) is relatively new on the international poetry arena, although to date he has contributed a number of poems to international and local poetry platforms, anthologies and magazines.
E: muzofafrancis@gmail.com
Twitter: @MuzofaFrancis

Paul R. Davis
(New York State, USA)

GONE

In a distant land across the sea,
a brilliant star has ascended
to claim her heavenly crown,
has given up her earthly reign
to be subject to God.
I aged with her, saw tragedy
and glory while this shining rock,
was more than rock, a monument
steadfast to the vagaries of time.
Today, I am visiting the lake
of my youth, so far yet close
in mind, and I will pray there
for a peace in my soul.
How very strange that
the stranger to me she
seemed to be in life
is now a friend and guide
in death. But friends
and guides never die,
and brilliant stars forever shine.

"I learned of her passing when I was undergoing a physical therapy treatment, and felt like my heart had been ripped out of me. I never kept up with her activities, but whenever I read about her in the news, I felt close to a good and almost saintly person. I heard her Christmas message during the Covid pandemic, and it made me feel optimistic and grateful for such a woman to express hope with such grace and humility. I feel fortunate to have had her in my life, albeit in perhaps a small way, but she will always be in my thoughts and in my heart."

~

ABOUT PAUL:
Paul's poetic philosophy is the joy of expression; the necessity of communication. His work has been published in *Chiron Review, Tipton Poetry Journal, Third Wednesday, The Externalist,* and many others.
E: 19suomi48@gmail.com

Charo Gabay Sidon
(SINGAPORE / PHILIPPINES)

KIND-HEARTED SOUL

Kind-hearted soul admired by
      many.
Touched many precious life.
She fought not only for her people
      but for everyone's peace and growth.
Her mission and vision is to helps people
      around the Globe!
Her gorgeous look the same with her
      beautiful heart.
Captivated by people hearts.
Adored by many people including me.
She smiles like an Angel and approachable
      person.
She is a loving mother of her children and and also to her Nation.
She built a strong foundation
Of love and respect to humanity
Blooming every single day
She is a extraordinary woman to be admired.
To be loved and to be respected.
She poured her life to served not only for her countrymen but all over
the world.
A strong Leader must follow and respect.
A queen with a kind heart.
Loved and Saluted by many.
A true precious gem that seldom in
      Universe had.
Hard to forget and will never be forgotten.
Her Majesty Queen Elizabeth II.

"My inspiration in writing this poem about Her Majesty Queen Elizabeth II are her good deeds and her humanity."

~

ABOUT CHARO:
Charo is a volunteer and domestic worker, and is one of the dedicated Team Leaders of Uplifters, a Non-Government Organisation offering online courses for migrant workers on Personal Growth, Mental Well-being, and Money management. She is also a volunteer

for the Centre for Domestic Employees, a Non-Government Organisation that aims to assist all domestic employees in Singapore. She has been writing poetry since a child, and has had a few of her poems published.
E: Sidoncharo9@gmail.com
FB: @aileen.gaba

Shabbirhusein K Jamnagerwalla
(TANZANIA)

FAREWELL TRIBUTE

The first glimpse that I had of this charismatic lady
Oh so many years ago was when I was hardly a matured man
She had come to Tanzania and she had come to St Alban's Church
I was lined up with my wife and other friends
Together with other thousands of curious on lookers awaiting her arrival
She was dressed as usual prettily with matching attires
With an epic matching hat atop her head
Holding an equally matching purse
Waving so heartily to everybody present there
Smiling so radiantly that the blushes on her cheeks appeared so vibrant
We had never seen such European flavor and beauty before
All whitey whitey and so attractive like the heavenly fairies
And her glistening eyes twinkled in delight and glow.

Yes she is our HM Queen Elizabeth II,
The darling of our dazzling times.
She has ruled Britain with unified visions
With hearty and humane jurisdiction and love for peace
Over the many decades of years.

Very sadly with grief in our hearts
Today we hear the passing away of the Queen Elizabeth II
A golden feather of our times has succumbed to the heavens
The whole World is besieged by this sad demise
We have so much sorrow and our uncontrollable tears
Are falling down our sopy cheeks
HM Queen Elizabeth II was an impeccable Angel of our times
Everyone has just one thing to impart upon this tragic departure
With trembling hands we lay down on the ground
The blossoming fragrant colorful flowers
In tribute to plenty of her outstanding attributes
That the World has of her majestic life
As we bid farewell of a colossal presence in our lives
HM Queen Elizabeth II rest in peace in your heavenly Abode.
Amen!

"I have been strangely drawn towards this lady since I was a mere lad. She had an awesome and lively flare that saw me always

attracted to her way of life, which was filled with elegance and morality. Yes, she was filled with a warmth and radiance that was a prize to watch out for. The passing away of this amazing lady has filled me with so much grief and sadness. Yet, I always say: Allah giveth; Allah taketh - we came to earth with nothing and go away with nothing! Rest in eternal peace, our queen!"

~

ABOUT SHABBIRHUSEIN:
Shabbirhusein has been writing poetry for the past 50 years. His Poems appear in: *Chaotic Times, Poets are Immortal, World Poetry Tree, Echoes of the African Drums, Bard's Day Keg, Peace Begins With Us, How To Write For Success, All I Want For Christmas, Williwash, My Pen & Soul, Be Literate* and others. He was honoured for literary excellence during India's 74th and 75th Independence celebrations, and is one of the 100 Global Recipients of Literary Honours, 2021-2022.
E: sitaronkajaan@gmail.com

Joseph Buehler.

(Georgia, USA)

FOURTEEN

When I was fourteen
my mother and I
attended a viewing of
Elizabeth II's coronation
on a black and white television

that was owned by an
Australian war bride. She
lived with her American
husband on an adjoining farm
in Michigan.

The Queen ruled for, as we
probably all know, seventy years.
She carried out her duties very well, even
up to two days before her death.
I've lived by now most of my life cognizant
of that undisputed fact.

"I've always admired the Queen's dedication to duty."

~

ABOUT JOSEPH:
Joseph has published over one hundred poems in over forty literary magazines including: *ArLiJo, The Tower Journal, Blue Bonnet Review, Serving House Journal, The Write Room, North Dakota Quarterly, Flatbush Review, Bumble Jacket Miscellany, The Opiate, Angry Old Man Magazine, Futures Trading, Ariel Chart, Nine Mile Magazine, Defenestration, Mad Swirl*, and others in the USA; *Sentinel Literary Quarterly* and *The Poet* in the UK; *Otoliths* in Australia; *Roi Faineant* and *H, C.E. Review* in Ireland; *Ottawa Arts Review* in Canada; and *Expanded Field* in the Netherlands.
E: josephbuehler@windstream.net

Shoshana Vegh

THE QUEEN OF ENGLAND

Her Majesty could have been
the Queen of Israel
but the last British soldier
left the Holy Land
when the British Mandate ended
a few years before they crowned Elizabeth –
she never had any time
between all the state ceremonies
to visit the Holy Land.

But when Israelis went shopping in London
they bought some symbols of royalty
simply missed having the manners of a queen
they wanted her to be theirs too
but the Queen did not visit –
the Land of Israel was
an unresolved matter
simply a boycott.

Legend has it that queens
hover over soldiers' graves
so now she must be visiting
the victorious dead of the First World War
buried on Mount Scopus in the Holy Land.

"*I live here in Israel and - in our past history - the British had a mandate and stayed here after the first world war, and the house of the King was, in a way, ruling life in Palestine before the establish of our country Israel. We still have places here that belong to the Royal family, and many British soldiers are buried on our land. We all love the monarchy, and respect the Queen; we visited as tourists and stood outside to look at the palace. England's charm was also for an Israeli.*"

~

ABOUR SOSHANA:
Shoshana wrote poetry and diaries from an early age, and has a master degree in Hebrew literature. Writing poetry started in the

wake of bereavement, when her brother Tuvia was killed in an accident during his military service in 1974. In 2000 she published her first novel, and in 2002 her second novel was published. She has gone onto publish and edit a large number of poetry and children's books, and founded a publishing house called *Pyutit* that specializes in publishing poetry books. She was awarded a scholarship from the House of the President of the State of Israel for her first poetry book *The Coming of Madness*, and from the Israel Foundation's scholarship for the book *Sad Ones*.

E: shoshs.vegh@gmail.com
FB: @Shoshana Vegh

Annamalai Muthusami
(INDIA)

ETCHED MEMORY
(She sways like a flower in the wind of our song)

She is not my neighbour
Not a co-walker, co-commuter
She is not close acquaintance
Not in same college or club
She is not personally seen
Not in any near proximity
She is not aware of me
Not like a drop in ocean
She is not heard of me
Not like a single note of symphony
Yet
She set a seal with indelible stamp
On my heart and soul.

At the pinnacle of majesty
At the state of the Queen regnant
At the pivot of world-authority
At the helm of universal sovereignty
At the peak of beloved excellency
At the plume of acknowledged highness
Not rather at their cost of
Colonial land and power,
She reigned realm of gold and gems
But the lives of loving human

We are familiar upon
Her portraits from age one
To the final and last at ninety-six
At all stages a glittering
Divinity and far elegance felt
Coping with blissful family and married life
Till passing away of her
"Better-whole" at ninety-nine.

Her charm and grace pervaded
Through all her ways and means
Her splendour and grandeur
Took gentle rhythm in all walks
Posh and delightfulness

Rush in every deed of her
Her handbag pochette, reticule
Or even colourful haversack
Are a source of sweet poems
Her Barbour waxed jacket,
And celebrated embroidered,
Beads intricately woven with
Deep- not light - coloured gowns etc.,
Flashed the shades of heaven

O, I am sure
World is not so bestowed
For a renewal of such being
In near future of thousand years ...
Yet, up to that period and beyond
We would remember, love and dote
Her etched memory in all.

"I have affectionately followed her motherly love for years, and felt heavy on the loss of her life, which set a strong impression of sorrowfulness in me."

~

ABOUT ANNAMALAI:
Annamalai has published five books of verse in Tamil. possesses post-graduate degrees in Engineering and English Literature, and served in the State Electricity Utility for many years.
E: anna.muthu21@gmail.com
E: acotel_edon@yahoo.co.in
Twitter: @Acotel.edon

Robert Leslie Fielding
(SCOTLAND / ENGLAND)

THE QUEEN

To us, Her Majesty Queen Elizabeth the Second was and remains our
queen.
To the world she was and remains The Queen.
The definite article indicates her uniqueness.
There was and will only ever be the one queen in all our lives.
Stars fade, politicos lose office, our Queen is and always will be The
Queen.
She has brought us from the lengthening post war days,
Through the clear and present danger of conflict, home and abroad.
Her presence has been the beacon that has lit our way,
Along the precarious paths of nationhood,
By the deep waters of international strife.
Picking her way for us to follow.
Retaining her dignity and impartiality,
Finding the stepping stones in the rushing rivers of life.
Ever reaching safety by her love for Jesus Christ, our Saviour.
Learning from Him that to lead is to serve.
She has been our servant for seventy years,
Years of challenge and turmoil,
Strife, domestic and international,
She has taught us that Love is the answer,
To whatever question asked of her.
This is her everlasting legacy to the world,
Love is the answer, the alpha and the omega,
Now and forever more.

*"Throughout my time abroad, I have remained a loyal subject of Her
Majesty, taking pride in all she has said and done for the nation, the
Commonwealth, for the world generally, and for British people in
particular. Those years in which she reigned over us were happy and
glorious. In penning this poem to the Queen, I has attempted to
define those special qualities so diligently and lovingly utilised by Her
Majesty in the course of her reign as Monarch of the United Kingdom
of Great Britain and Northern Ireland. I am a devoted subject now of
King Charles the Third."*

~

ABOUT ROBERT:

Robert has been a centre lathe turner in Manchester, and an English Language Lecturer at universities in Britain and overseas. He has had three books published, along with blogs and e-zine articles containing hundreds of thousands of words, written for students of English, as well as for general readership.

FB: @robert.l.fielding

Ann Privateer
(California, USA)

MY STUDY

Before TV there was radio
The family huddled near it
Listening to world news
England and the Queen

In college I was an English major
Victorian Lit to be specific
Queen Elizabeth the first
Was everything to me

Time passes and I got to know
Queen Elizabeth the second
My whole life, she was there
In the background checking me

Seventy years changing yet
Remaining the same, my family
Spent a summer in England
We walked in her parks with love.

"During the time when I was watching television footage of the Queen's funeral, I happened upon this envelope that I have treasured for many years with Queen Elizabeth's face, and was inspired to write this poem."

~

ABOUT ANN:
Ann is a poet, artist, and photographer. Her work has appeared in a number of publications including: *Third Wednesday, Entering* and *MindFull.*
E: annprivateer@gmail.com
Instagram: @annershea

Ion-Marius Tatomir
(ENGLAND / ROMANIA)

GUIDANCE FROM ABOVE

Thousand years will be gone, and many other thousands,
will pass away carried by the oceans of time,
but the glory of Your reign will never fade,
thy splendour will shine through the ages,
inspiring, igniting and leading ...
Your dedicated work for an united nation
remains inscribed in history with golden letters
and in the heart of a whole world the admiration,
for everything You did without hesitation.
Passing through the rainbow gate, You send us light and guidance,
to do our best for the world and the society,
we will never cess to say, while looking at the sky,
where now You belong to the amazing starry infinity,
with tears in eyes and gratitude: Thank You, Your Majesty!

"Her Majesty was part of our lives; always active and engaged in work for a better world. She will always inspire, and remains an example for us to follow and to do our best wherever we are. Through my poem I wanted to express this thought, this reality, and my gratitude."

~

ABOUT ION-MARIUS:
Ion-Marius made his poetic debut in Phoenix New Life poetry (England), where he had poems published from 2004 to 2008. From 2005 to the present he is periodically published in *Metverse Muse* international poetry anthology, (India). In 2006 his volume of poetry *Stars and Flowers* was published. In 2010 he was included in *A Dictionary of Contemporary International Poets* (China), and in 2013, in the *Anthology of the Romanian Contemporary Writers Worldwide* (Romania). Also published in: *Kitob Dunyasi*, (Uzbekistan, 2021); and *Galaxy-Anthology of Contemporary Poetry*, (Italy, 2021). He has also been published in France in the poetry anthologies: *Terre en poesie* (2007), *Paix et Fraternite en poesie* (2009), *Sourire et Amitie en poesie* (2013), *Tendresse en poesie* (2014), *Nuit et jour en poesie* (2015), *Amour en poesie* (2016), *Soleil et Lune en Poesie* (2021).
E: tatomir@gmail.com

Cathy Hailey
(Virginia, USA)

LOOKING FORWARD AND LOOKING BACK

After a business trip in London in the sixties,
Dad brought my brother a gift of toy soldiers–tiny
replicas of the Queen's Royal Guards marching
in red jackets, black pants and bearskin hats.

Dad brought me a magical blue-eyed doll dressed
in royal violet velveteen, soft to the touch, bejeweled,
blond locks haloed in purple, complementary,
Lily-of- the-Valley bouquet held in delicate hands.

My brother's toy soldiers came alive in the seventies
during study abroad, when I lived on Queen's Gate.
Soldiers marched stiff-legged in unison as I watched
the changing of the guard at Buckingham Palace.

I played tour guide on honeymoon in the eighties
following past footsteps to recreate my temporary
London citizenship for my husband–sharing tea and pints,
castles and palace, soldiers marching in red and black.

Now a sadness falls over their joyful royal red.
I see them daily as they carry out Queen Elizabeth's
wishes while the world mourns, celebrates her life,
raises questions–looking forward and looking back.

"As I witnessed coverage of Queen Elizabeth's death and funeral, I found myself looking back to my time living in London as a study-abroad student, and thinking about keepsakes connected to the Queen – a doll that reminds me of a youthful queen, toy soldiers in the likeness of her Royal Palace Guards. My mother is 91, and I see parallels between her and Queen Elizabeth because of the events they've witnessed. I admire the Queen, but hearing about the protests against the monarchy and colonialism, I can't help but look forward with hope that the UK and the US will reckon with their histories and improve their democracies."

~

ABOUT CATHY:

Cathy teaches as an adjunct lecturer in Johns Hopkins University's online MA in Teaching Writing program, and previously taught high-school English and Creative Writing. She is Northern Region Vice President of The Poetry Society of Virginia, co-hosts Virginia Voices, hosts Where Art Meets the Line, and organizes In the Company of Laureates. Her writing has been published in *The New Verse News, Poetry Virginia, Written in Arlington, Stay Salty: Life in the Garden State (Vol. 2), Poetry for Ukraine, Family,* and *NoVA Bards.* Poems are forthcoming in *The Poetry Society of Virginia Centennial Anthology.* Her chapbook, *I'd Rather Be a Hyacinth* is due for release early 2023.

E: haileycp@gmail.com
W: www.cathyhailey.com
FB: @cathy.hailey.5
Instagram: @haileycp
Twitter: @haileycp

Cheryl-Iya Broadfoot
(ENGLAND / SOUTH AFRICA)

TO BE A QUEEN (THANK YOU MA'AM)

To be a queen is to hold your head high, keep your feet
firmly on the ground
To be The Queen one has to be seen in order
to be believed
To be a queen is being able to switch off at five pm and
play with the kids
To be The Queen is to be on duty twenty-four-seven
with your kids in tow

To be a queen is to determine
your own success
To be The Queen is to determine
a country's success
To be a queen is to retire at sixty-seven and
travel the world in peace
To be The Queen is to travel the world brokering peace
until your ninety-six

To be a queen is hard enough
To be The Queen is quite extreme

So hold your head high,
keep your feet on the ground
Be seen,
be believed and
be serving your dreams
and always
be a queen

Leader, pioneer, way shower
Monarch, mother, matriarch
Thank you Ma'am
for paving the way
for all women
to be a queen

*"Inspired by the dedication of the Queen, and the way she has been a
role model for women as leaders, this poem celebrates the path the
Queen carved that allows all other women to lead and inspire those
who follow through the ranks of life."*

~

ABOUT CHERYL-LYA:

Cheryl-lya is an avid Soul Adventurer. Her first adventures began in the classroom, daydreaming instead of learning, writing and poetry were always secret loves … Chocolate and tea-lover, usually found helping women launch successful and sustainable businesses, she has been known to caress the realms of the typed-word occasionally (as a novice).

W: www.soulscompass.net
FB: @cheryllya.broadfoot
Twitter: @souls_compass
Amazon Author Page: @B006TYZV3C

Francie Scanlon
(New York State, USA)

OLD AGE COMETH TO THOSE WHO SERVE AND ALSO WAIT

Who toll in the vineyard of History
Hoping to meet the moment rise to the occasion tackling their Destiny.
No footballer ever has or ever will more deftly soar the score on the board.
Rattle the opposition by exposing their vain-glorious ineptitude
Or wrestle the challenges of Life, personal and public, with greater dignity aloft.

"Her Majesty the Queen" knew intimately Life's vicissitudes.
She understood poignantly and steadfastly her appointed role without a second of flight but rather formidable embrace.
Never swerving from the mantle of the Monarch's monumentally.
She is now forever enshrined as a monument herself of 'steady as you go', gumption and glory.

Oh, fear not: God saved the Queen, over and over, every day of her ninety-six years for the benefit of the Commonwealth and all who believe in the sanctity of the Sovereign purpose.

Fate has been faithful to the Queen.
The undying, unquenchable loyalty of the People will out-distance momentary vagaries and tumult thereby advancing the Legacy of the Queen.

The Queen lives forever in memory, in might, and in the earnestness of her magnificent goodwill to all.

"My life-changing encounter with Queen Elizabeth occurred on the Queen's second visit to New York City, July, 1976, when she was decreed a Citizen of New York. I had the joy of beholding the Queen in glorious lime green, en route to Bloomingdale's in an open motorcade."

~

ABOUT FRANCIE:
Francie's published by-line articles have appeared in *Newsday, W,*

The Irish Echo, Brooklyn Daily Eagle and other publications.
Instagram: @hintfair

Shereen Abraham
(UNITED ARAB EMIRATES / INDIA)

A QUEEN LIKE NO OTHER

As a queen you were truly incomparable
What you did for your country is unforgettable
For seven decades you made a difference
With elegance, diligence and perseverance.

You were a queen like no other
You were both tough and tender
You were sweet, gentle and kind
Your dedication blew my mind.

What made you so special?
Was it your smile?
Your sense of style?
Your charm?
Your empathy?
Your grace?
Your charisma?
Your open-mindedness?
Your selflessness?
Your devotion to duty?
Your courage?
Your resilience?
Your humility?
Your faith?
Your sense of humour?
Your thoughtfulness?
Your compassion?
What was it?

You will always remain an inspirational queen
You were not just a queen, you were The Queen
Perhaps the reason why your passing gave me pain
Even though I was never under your reign!

"The Queen was such an inspiration to me, and when she passed I felt a deep sense of loss, even though I was never under her reign."

~

ABOUT SHEREEN:

Shereen is a writer, artist, happiness coach, soft-skills trainer, theta healer, and devotee of all things creative. Over the years she has written articles and poems that have been published in a number magazines and anthologies. She finds inspiration in the life that surrounds her ... simple things like music, the sights, sounds & smell of nature, the colours & aroma of food, people and their fleeting emotions.

E: shereen.abraham@gmail.com
Instagram: @ShereenAbrahamArt

Shakti Pada Mukhopadhyay
(INDIA)

AN ELEGY OF REMINISCENCE

Even as a child, Lilibet communicated
to the people of UK during the Second World War,
expressing her pains for the sufferings of the children.
At the age of 25, sudden death of her father compelled her
to adorn herself with the crown of the Queen,
she might not have foreseen.

To her country men Queen Elizabeth II set a unique example,
by broadcasting the Coronation ceremony live.
From the very beginning she wished to lead
a purposeful and an un- ostentatious life.
She had danced with the President of Ghana and raised
her voice against colour-bar and apartheid.

Her novel gesture prompted Ghana
to continue as a Commonwealth country.
To show solidarity with her country men
she helped BBC to telecast a documentary
in 1969, named "Royal Family",
showing day-to- day protocols of the Queen's family.

Her popularity graph touched its peak
at that time among her country men.
For eminence of her family and country,
she didn't hesitate to bypass the protocols then.
To common men her opinions she started to share
in Australia and New Zealand on her visits there .

She was displeased when the Romanian dictator
Nicolae Ceauşescu was invited to visit her country.
She succeeded in projecting herself as the
guardian of a country. In the year two thousand twenty
she alerted for the Covid calamities,
similar to the Second World War tragedies.

But as a stateswoman she concluded her speech
with a ray of hope, providing a solace in,
"We'll meet again ... we'll meet again ...,"
from the song of Vera Lynn.

The demise of the Queen who witnessed
10 heads of France, 13 heads of her country,
and 14 heads of India and USA,
has created a vacuum as a trustee
and pathfinder for the people of her own country.

On her visit to India in 1961, she expressed,
"It is no secret that there have been
some difficult episodes in our past,
Jallianwala Bagh … is a distressing
example … We must learn from the sadness
and build on the gladness."

On her demise, a shadow of grief pervaded many regions,
cutting the barriers of race and religions.

"Queen Elizabeth II's life and actions are praiseworthy. As a human being, she exhibited finer qualities of acknowledging difficult and distressing episodes of the past, learning from the sadness and raising voice against colour-bar, apartheid and dictatorship. She was also a competent stateswoman."

~

ABOUT SHAKTI:
Shakti has been published in a number of international magazines and journals including: *Borderless, Passager, Molecule, Better Than Starbucks, Tatkhanik, The Dribble Drabble Review, The Poet, Deep Overstock, MindFull, CafeLitMagazine, Down in the Dirt, Academy of the Heart and Mind*. His writings have also been accepted for publication in *Muse India,* and *Scarlet Leaf Review*.
E: shaktimukherjee.synbank@gmail.com

Tyson West
(Massachusetts, USA)

HER PREFERRED REALM

Though she wore outfits modern, smart and bright
she seemed a tourist from a bygone age
where Nanny's rules of etiquette would swage
the firstborn girl into an uptight sprite.

Becoming princess with her uncle's flight
Liz vowed her lifetime service on war's stage.
When she wore outfits modern, smart and bright
she muttered maxims from a bygone age.

Once royal pomp resolved, her shy delight
would trot to stables where she would engage,
old coat and head scarf, her groom to assuage
the piebald's flank. With joy she flexed her might
here free from outfits modern, smart and bright.

"I was inspired to write this rondel when I saw an interview on television showing the Queen's friendship with a California cowboy who she invited to work with her horses in England. The cowboy recalled when he first met this monarch famous for her colorful outfits, she wore a plain coat and headscarf. He thought she was a groom. Elizabeth and the cowboy bonded over their love of horses."

~

ABOUT TYSON:
Tyson writes free verse, Asian micro verse, including haiku and tanka, and form poetry.
E: purplelynx2000@yahoo.com

Igor Pop Trajkov
(NORTH MACEDONIA)

100 YEARS IN 1 DAY

Nobody knew it could strike us so much...
While lying on the shore
So young and happy so much
Indecisive of our future
Suddenly the sun disappeared
Those big metal ravens started
Waving. We all saw the disappearances
Of everything we cared about.
This thing is called war- innocence
Is disappearing then - that is how they
Told us. We wanted to ask something
More, all this seemed so sudden
For us. Somebody was reading
Something on the radio, I remember
We all went to fight those dark grey
Birds... In the years before new
Attitudes began, as Lady Houston
Said: When the truth is told at Wavertree
Wavertree will set India free.
They all changed, our Best
Even gave Randolph[1] to Tito,
From the Balkans I still have
My pen friend. After all of it
We had You on our side.
Today I saw You were gone.
Am I gone too, after all those
Hundreds of years, or am I all
Alone? Certainly not, it is obvious
Eternity exists, though there's
No proof for it. Today the bravest
Of us—all that were and will be
Eternal—are having our feast
Celestial, with the bravest
Recipes of our beliefs.

"I always believed in democracy, as I always believed that the necessity of aristocracy is undeniable. Queen Elisabeth was a brave sovereign, and found out from my grandfather and his friends about her role in during WWII. Queen Elisabeth was very popular in the *region where I am from. For us from our region, she will always remain as someone fighting against the dark side. I think she deserves our thankfulness for many things, which is why I decided to pay her tribute."*

~

ABOUT IGOR:
Igor is a prolific writer across all genres of literature, including theory and journalism. His work has been translated into many languages, and has participated in a large number of international events. He has won a number of awards for his work including: The Best Christmas Message Contest (2020), organized by American Corner Struga, and the best poem contest of Healthy Options Project Skopje (2021), for the Day of the Fight Against the Drugs, with his poem *Body Double*.
E: igorpoptrajkov@yahoo.com
W: www.pyramidusd.wordpress.com
FB: @Igor Pop Trajkov (Luka)
Instagram: @trajkovpop

Keith Burton
(California, USA)

HEAVEN

Entering heaven,
She was greeted by Jesus,
And all the saints.

A choir of cherubs sang hallelujahs,
As the heavenly host styled her,
"The Perfect Queen."

So great was the press,
Angels folded their wings,
To keep from crushing their pinions.

For none had endured so much,
Sacrificed so long,
Nor given such love to a nation.

Elizabeth Rex was grace incarnate,
"The Jewel Who Wore a Crown",
For 70 blessed years.

"Although I'm an American, I spent second and third form in a British boarding school in the '60s. I had, and continue to have, the greatest respect for Queen Elizabeth, and the wonderful example of service she set for the world."

~

ABOUT KEITH:
As a musician, Keith has performed throughout the US, and his poems have appeared worldwide. He was honoured to have met Mother Theresa, and the Dalai Lama.
E: keith1080@gmail.com

Aminath Neena
(ENGLAND / MALDIVES)

ODE TO THE QUEEN OF HEARTS

How many of us have heard
Of a woman who hoisted the bulky flag
Of sovereignty at the tender age
of only a score and a quarter?

When flowers bloomed in spring
And the butterflies grooved around
She went on taming the horses

How many of us have heard
Of a woman who held on to obligations
with faith, wisdom and diligence
for seven decades or so?

When kings and rulers chanted
"Look at me, I am the sovereign here!"
Her invisible aura enchanted all

How many of us have heard
Of a woman whose silhouette withered
the storms of passing seasons and continued
till the final whistle of this journey?

When the last of the *lily of the valleys* of summer
whispered "take us with you, your majesty"
They laid some, on her final resting place

"Just like many Maldivians, Queen Elizabeth has been a familiar figure to me from a very early age. Although, I have never seen her in person, I hold a lot of admiration and respect for her in my heart. I remember my mother telling me of the Queen's visit to the Maldives in 1972. She recalls the grandeur and the celebrations that were held during this particular visit. May she rest in peace."

~

ABOUT AMINATH:
Aminath is an English lecturer. An avid lover of words, poetry is a hobby closest to her heart. Her poems usually revolve around themes

such as love, relationships, spirituality, society, and global issues. According to her, poetry is the gateway to spirituality because it resonates purity like no other. Her poems are published or are forthcoming in a range of international platforms including: *Trouvaille Review, Spill words, Muddy River Poetry Review, Impspired magazine, Continue the voice magazine* and *Borderless Journal*. Her poems also have been published in anthologies including: *Eccentric Orbits* by Dimensionfold publishing, and *Poetica 2* of Clarendon House publications. Aminath has also been nominated for the 2022 Pushcart Prize for her poem *Dystopia*. She has an MA TESOL from the University of Nottingham, and has recently published her poetry collection *Dreams of my heart.*
E: aminathneenahanyf@gmail.com

Minko Tanev
(BULGARIA)

LAST GOODBYE
TO HER MAJESTY QUEEN ELIZABETH II

The era of the Queen ends,
with inscribed profile of Her Majesty
on postage stamps and coins.
Her 70 years of service to Great Britain
is sign with the kilometer-long rows of tributes.

Endless hours of waiting and personal reflection.
Farmers take off their hats from afar.
Ceremonial trumpets and cannon volleys
mark the ritual.
Military airplanes mark Her star path.

The crown reaches a diamond jubilee
and bears the weight of history
with countless humanitarian missions,
with prayers that God bless us all.
The spirit empire has been like a fairy tale.

A life devoted to God and duty
elevates Her into a symbol of the monarchy.
Dignity forever records
Her name in the book of honor
with the aura of a queen.

An era of fanfare is passing

"The poem was written for participation in World Birland Poets Poetry Tribute To H.R.M. Queen Elizabeth II, at the invitation of H.R.H. Princess Prof. Eden S. Trinidad. And with deep respect and reverence for the life and work of H.R.M. Queen Elizabeth II."

~

ABOUT MINKO:
Minko is a Philologist of the Bulgarian language. He is the author of six books of poetry, and co-author of three bilingual books, poetry and haiku. He is in the European Top 100 of the most creative haiku, and editor of over 70 books. He has also participated in a large

number of anthologies and editions, with numerous awards and recognition around the world including the Chinese International Zhengxin Poet Award (2022).

E: minkotanev@abv.bg
FB: @Minko Tanev

Julie Bonner Williams
(Michigan, USA)

TEA WITH THE QUEEN

My English friend Tonia
stood beside me at the gates of
Buckingham Palace where we peered
through the December night and iron bars
from a London sidewalk

The flag is flying, Tonia noted, t*he Queen is in.*

I imagined Her Majesty
in a pink wool suit and equally pink shoes in
a sprawling, lamp-lit apartment where shadows
flickered on crystal vases beneath a portrait of
King Charles I on regal wallpaper above a carved
table with framed photographs of a woman
in scarf and Wellies,
Corgis at her ankles

I pictured Her Royal Majesty
seated in a petit point chair, sippping
perfect tea from a delicate, rose-stenciled
cup, its rim tipped with gold and
thought of her nibbling the edges of
chocolate HobNobs when no one
was watching

At the gift shop inside
Buckingham Palace
I bought a box of handkerchiefs
in assorted prints: polka dots
and stripes and paisley
print for my grandfather and
at Christmas mailed them to his Detroit
apartment where, years later, I
saw them again the afternoon I arrived
to box up his life, making way
for the next tenant

The handkerchiefs were pristine; unopened
cellophane tape still on the box I wrapped
years before, attaching a card reading,

"I bought these at Buckingham Palace!"

It was then I realized what a silly
gift it was - my grandfather carried a plain,
white handkerchief every day of
his life - he would never use
anything 'too nice.'

"After writing to a pen pal on Isle of Wight, England, from the age of fifteen, I flew to England thirteen years later to spend a week with her. I returned to England two years later to be maid of honor at my friend's wedding. This poem is a true account of seeing Buckingham palace for the first time. Hearing Queen Elizabeth II was in, I imagined what the Queen might be doing right then. I really did buy a box of handkerchiefs for my grandfather, and found them unopened years later. As I was recently teaching a class in the college where I'm an English professor, a student announced that the Queen had just died. In the front row of that class sat a student from England. He stood, excused himself, and left the room. He returned a few minutes later and said, 'God Save the Queen.' I sensed how alone he felt, hearing this news away from home and those who truly grasped the magnitude of her passing."

~

ABOUT JULIE:
Julie is a writer and English professor living on the lakeshore with her husband, three dogs, three cats, twenty-six chickens, two horses, and a mule named Amos. She is an avid gardener and has a small, organic lavender farm. Her interests include collecting antiques, reading, and amassing ridiculous amounts of Bic Cristal pens and legal pads.
FB: Julie Bonner Williams Author

Chris Nedahl
SPAIN / WALES

RAINBOW QUEEN

Red roses and berries
Orange pumpkins and autumn
Yellow sun and sand
Green emeralds and leaves
Blue skies and seas
Indigo horizons and plums
Violet aubergines and amethysts

Reflections of a rainbow
in every queenly task
and radiant smile
spectrum hues
for every duty
joyous or solemn
her measure befitting.

"I have been inspired to write a number of poems expressing my thoughts on Queen Elizabeth's life and death. I think of her as a queen for all seasons, a constant for the UK and Commonwealth throughout her amazing reign."

~

ABOUT CHRIS:
Chris writes about anything and everything. Micro fiction, flash fiction and poetry are current favourites. Published internationally in anthologies, print and online, she is working on compiling a book of her poetry. On becoming an expat in Spain, she was an active and appreciative member of Writers Abroad until it folded, and is now delighted to be a part of Pens Around The World, a group of expats writing and critiquing together whilst living across the world.
W: www.christinenedahl.wordpress.com

Pankhuri Sinha
(INDIA)

FOR THE QUEEN

There is a picture of yours
Your highness, of you
Laughing out loud, in the
Face of adversity
In Challenging times
With clouds of war
Gathering and hovering
Not continental but spanning the world!

Of course, some might
Say, to look for beauty
With death around
Is brutal! But some one
Needs to command
Has to energize
Not just the troops
Standing to beat death
With bare hands
But those at home
Safeguarding all
For which wars are fought!

That picture, along with
A grave posture in
An off shoulder dress
Bedecked with
Jewels and the Crown
Of the official coronation
Beams of royalty!

At 25, only, you looked regal!

Point is all these images
Inspire women regardless
Of country, marital status
Sitting in their public
Or private offices!

The multiple, the myriad
Problems endlessly

Appearing in front of
Today's women
Modernized, liberated partially
Need an inspiration no less
Than you! Your Highness !

"I was a student of History, specializing in British Imperialism, and so the death of the Queen felt like a personal event, a turning point in history. The Queen with her hard work has drawn the attention and admiration of many in the former colonies and the current commonwealth group, and my poem emphasises this, as well as highlighting how the female monarch embodied woman power, inspiring women across race and citizenship."

~

ABOUT PANKHURI:
Pankhuri is a bilingual poet, story writer and translator. She has two poetry collections published in English, two story collections published in Hindi, six poetry collections published in Hindi, and many more are lined up. She has been translated in over 27 languages, and published in many journals and anthologies, both at home and abroad. Pankhuri has also won a number of prestigious, national and international awards including: the Girija Kumar Mathur Award, the Chitra Kumar Shailesh Matiyani Award, the Seemapuri Times Rajeev Gandhi Excellence Award, and First prize for poetry by Rajasthan Patrika.
E: nilirag18@gmail.com

Prof. Mushtaque Ahmed Pathan
(PAKISTAN)

THE LOVING QUEEN

The great lady of the land
World claps with the hand
Salute your Majesty
Salute your dynasty
And symbol of wisdom
You ran the kingdom
With love and harmony
Among all the clans
With your nice plans
Plans developed the country
In education and technology
With peace and prosperity
Grew the nation to high rise
With your vision wise
You will be remembered for centuries
In the world and countries
Countries you ruled in
Countries you liberated
With international gesture
With good deeds and culture
UK remains a world power
By your love and shower
People miss you great
A lady with imperial hat
Hats off to you

"Her Majesty Queen Elizabeth is a world famous personality who ruled for more than half century, and brought peace and prosperity to her country, and deserves high tribute."

~

ABOUT MUSHTAQUE:
Mushtaque is a Professor of Geology at the University of Sindh, Jamshoro. He loves poetry, people and nature, and writes poems on various topics and issues.
E: mapathan@usindh.edu.pk

Margareth Stewart
(ENGLAND / BRAZIL / ITALY)

MAJESTICALLY

She bowed majestically
Taking the teacup
Unhurriedly drank it
Her favourite drink, has been always
The 'Lady grey,'
Her favourite sky,
Colour.

She came to reign
Her kingdom started so early
She assumed it with dedication
Despite her youth, her second thoughts
Her body and soul bowed to it
Her gin and tonic kept her faithfulness

Like a young old person,
She grew younger with age,
Being a queen, standing on
Well-polished shoes
Facing all circumstances,
Sign of perseverance

Whatever comes ...
Whatever goes ...
Destined to grow!

Whoever saw,
Her Majesty
Would have no idea
Of how many rows are needed
To keep the boat from sinking

The presence of a kingdom
In the veins of a country
Royalty, her loyalty
Shining high

No one thinks
Queens ever end
An empty throne stands

Her castle feels like solitude
The fairy tale is over
Too mundane to bear

Out of humanities
Born we are
Carrying the Queen
With brave hearts
Emblem of her choice
Even with the cost
Of her own Majesty
The Queen

"This poem is deeply related to my love and esteem for Queen Elisabeth II and her Kingdom, and also for being a female leader who stayed the longest in power."

~

ABOUT MARGARETH:
Currently a visiting professor at The University of York in the Department of English and Related Literature. Margareth Stewart is the pen name of Monica Mastrantonio, lecturer and researcher in the field of Social Psychology. She combines her passion for the literary world with scientific inquisitions in order to develop words and writings that are deeply engaged in activism and equality. She has published the following novels: *Open/Pierre's journey after WW2, Mademoiselle-sur-Seine*, and *Urban Poems*. *Zero Chance* is her new thriller for the next season. Right now, she is developing a series in partnership with a Pakistan author.
Instagram: @ author_margarethstewart
Twitter: @Mastrantonio

Stoianka Boianva
(BULGARIA)

COMMEMORATING
HER MAJESTY QUEEN ELIZABETH II

September winds carry Her soul away.
Lilies of the valley ring with weeping small bells.
The world says goodbye to the worthy Queen.

Scottish bagpipes sound soulfully.
Church choir and angel chants.
Prayers and divine messages.
The sound of fanfare echoed across London.
Silence. And worship. And thoughts.

Big Ben is in mourning and beats every minute.
Guardsmen, citizens, state leaders, the family.
Multitude solemnly walks.
The million screens send Her -
with sadness and love, with cannon salutes,
they recall events from Her reign.

Angelic songs welcome Her.
Heaven's rainbows rise in illumination.
Fly to stars, galaxies, glistening universes.
Her loved ones are waiting for Her in heaven.
Farewell to a Great Earthly Kingdom.
Reaching the Kingdom of Divine Love.

"The poem was written with deep respect and reverence for the life and work of H.R.M. Queen Elizabeth II, and for participation in World Birland Poets Poetry Tribute to H.R.M. QUEEN ELIZABETH II, at the invitation of H.R.H. Princess Prof. Eden S. Trinidad."

~

ABOUT STOIANKA:
Stoianka is a physicist. Chairwoman of Haiku Club (Plovdiv), she is the author of twelve books, the co-author of three bilingual books of poetry and haiku, and edits a number of dictionaries and publications. She is in the European Top 100 of the most creative haiku authors.
E: stboianova@abv.bg
FB: @Stoianka Boianova

END

www.THEPOETMagazine.org

Printed in Great Britain
by Amazon

87039818R00102